Write Mindfully
Unlocking the writer within

Rebecca Lowe

This book is sold subject to the condition that it shall not, by way of trade or otherwise, be lent, re-sold, hired out or otherwise circulated without the publisher's prior consent in any form of binding or cover other than that in which it is published and without a similar condition being imposed on the subsequent purchaser.

Cover Illustration: FuuJ @fuuj via Unsplash. Published under Unsplash Creative Commons license, June 2024.

Copyright © 4 June 2024 Rebecca Lowe

Published by Talisman Arts

All rights reserved.

ISBN : 9798326906267

'We come whirling out of nothingness, scattering stars like dust...The stars made a circle and in the middle, we dance'.
— Rumi.

'My work is loving the world, which is mostly standing still and learning to be astonished'.
— Mary Oliver.

DEDICATION

For my daughter, Stephanie, my greatest inspiration.
Keep singing your own, beautiful song.

With grateful thanks to all my friends and fellow artists, who have supported and encouraged me over the years.

Soli Deo Gloria

CONTENTS

1. Fear of the blank page — 20
2. Listen with your eyes — 34
3. The seeds of creativity — 48
4. Inspiration or perspiration? — 62
5. Writing is breathing — 77
6. Ditch the pebble in your shoe — 86
7. Creative playfulness — 112
8. The power of storytelling — 130
9. The singer not the song — 148
10. Finding your flow — 161
11. Senses and sensibility — 172
12. Writing the self — 184
13. Beauty will save the world — 193

APPENDIX: Manifesto, The Affirmations and Wombwell Rainbow Interview — 200

PREFACE

Chyma

In the beginning, before even time existed, there was the Voice of the Divine hovering over the waters, a shaking of everything into motion.

In the beginning was the Word...
Spoken into being,
Sung into being,
Reverberated,
Resonant.

I have seen words spin over waters. They look like flowers or mandalas or the spinning axis of the planets. It looks a lot like creative intelligence.

In the beginning was a word which loved itself so much it longed to be spoken, it longed to be sung. So it sang itself into being. In the beginning was spelling, musical enchantment. En-chant, from chant, which means 'to sing'. A resonance of not one note, but many, some beyond the register of hearing, which sang, not to be heard but for the sheer joy of being alive.

In the beginning was breath – ruach – a divine pneuma. Wind-spirit – breathed, inspired into every living thing, breathed so gently, almost imperceptibly, a vibrational energy that made things spin, that set into motion every single thing.

In the beginning, a single molecule felt that drive to create and recreate, to divide and sub-divide into Vesica Pisces, two halves splitting and splitting, until flowers blossomed, seeds and flowers of life craving itself, incarnating, eternal and infinitesimal. Until – bones hardened, hearts pumped into being, until – life in all its fullness, all its glory and variety sprang into generous, glorious being!

And all of this, *all* of this – from a single voice, a whisper over the waters,

A Song,

A Breath,

A Word.

INTRODUCTION

'The hardest part of any journey is having the confidence to start'.
– Round-the-world cyclist Mark Beaumont.

Welcome! I'm guessing if you are reading this book, you are a creative person like me, maybe a writer, an artist or a musician (or perhaps all three!). Perhaps you have always been creative, ever since you were a child. Or maybe you came to it later in life and want to know how to do more. Whoever you are, and whatever your circumstances, you are very welcome here. I hope we can journey together and become friends, growing in our creativity and confidence, and sparking off new ideas along the way.

I am writing this book for others, like me, who wish to become more creative and also more mindful. Most of all, I'm writing it for anyone who has ever felt the urge to create but is afraid of getting it wrong or doesn't know where to start. If you go to poetry nights and find yourself saying 'Of course, I love poetry, but I'm not really a poet' or visit art galleries and say 'I loved painting when I was little but I'm not good enough to be an artist'. If you've ever felt yourself confined to the edges of the world's dancefloor watching others strutting their stuff and reminiscing fondly about the days when you, too, used to dance like nobody was watching... then this book is for you.

A warning:

There are several things this book won't do. It won't:

- Turn you into a best-selling author
- Tell you how to get your work published and/or make money out of it
- Show you how to write (only you can do that)

There are lots of books already out there that do these things. If you want to become a top-selling, top-earning professional author (and good luck to you, genuinely) go and buy one of those books.

Instead, this book aims to help you find and listen to your inner voice – your Soul Voice, if you like. Once you can do so, you will find that writing comes naturally to you – as naturally as breathing.

'But I'm not a writer!'

This is one of the most common complaints I hear in any of the workshops I run. A lot of people are afraid that if they label themselves as a writer they will be compared unfavourably with 'proper writers'. It does sound arrogant, doesn't it, to give myself the same title as, say, Dylan Thomas or Shakespeare or TS Eliot?! But every writer had to start somewhere, and even successful writers go through many drafts and face countless rejections before finding success. Jane Austen's early draft of Pride and Prejudice was rejected by London publishing firm Cadell &Davies in 1797 and left to languish on the author's desk for another sixteen years before it was finally published by Thomas Egerton in 1813. JK Rowling's Harry Potter series was rejected by twelve different publishing houses before becoming an international best-seller. So just because your work isn't hitting the best-sellers lists doesn't mean you are not a writer.

What is a writer? Simple. **A writer is someone who writes**. An artist is someone who makes art. A musician is someone who makes music. If you do any of these things, you qualify. You have earned the title of artist already.

'But anyone could do what I do...'

Here's one I've heard lots of times. I'm equally guilty of it. Perhaps it's because of competitive shows like The Voice and The X Factor but we seem to think that, in order to be an artist, you have to be better than everybody else. Well, here's a secret: You don't. I was never very keen on art at school, but in recent years I've started drawing and painting Celtic art. I love the way the shapes and patterns curl and flow into one another, and drawing them makes me deeply satisfied. I'm not a brilliant artist. I make art because I enjoy it. For a long time, I hid my paintings away. I was frightened that if I started showing them to people, they might be disparaging. I felt like a fraud. What if somebody came up to me and said 'That's rubbish! Anyone could do that!' Or, even worse, 'My six-year-old child could do that!'? It was the same with my writing. I loved creating poetry but whenever I received another rejection from a literary magazine or was unplaced in a poetry competition, it felt like a slap across the face. I grew deeply jealous of the success of other poets, even to the point of resolving not to write any more. Then I realised how ridiculous I was being. Of course, a lot of people could paint or write just as well as me if they wanted to. A lot of them could paint and write better. But the fact is that I am doing it. It's not about seeking others' approval. It's the act of creating, of leaving my mark upon the world. These days, if somebody came up to me and said 'but I could paint that just as well' my response would be 'Brilliant! I'm glad I have inspired you – now go and do it!' Life is not a competition. You don't have to be the best, or the best-selling, or the most successful. That's not what creativity is for.

I was watching a TV programme a while ago about child prodigies. There was a little girl, aged about nine, who was brilliant on the piano. She was amazing, truly gifted. Yet listening to her performances, there was something missing. Yes, technically they were brilliant, but when she played she was totally static, like a machine, with no emotion. When asked after her concert why she liked playing the piano, she answered 'Because I can win competitions'. She had been gifted with the most amazing ability, yet somehow nobody had taught her the whole purpose of the music, which is uplift the spirit, to bring yourself and others joy.

'But I'm not good enough!'

Here's another secret: The more you do something, the better you will get at it. When I was living in London, I went to visit an exhibition by the artist Cezanne, most famous for his painting of the Saint-Victoire Mountain. Did you know that he painted that same mountain over 60 times? And that's just the ones we know about. I wonder how many more potential masterpieces ended up crumpled up in litterbins because their creator wasn't quite happy with them?

In fact, scientists have come up with the exact formula for how much work you need to put in, in order to become good at something. They determined that it took exactly 10,000 hours of practice to become an expert in any field – be it learning a new language, training for a sport, or mastering a musical instrument. Broken down, that's around 20 hours a week over 10 years, or about two hours a day.[i] But even if you can't afford a full two hours (and let's be honest, few of us can!), just a few minutes each day will make a big difference.
While we might not all be a Mozart or a Beethoven in the making, it stands to reason that when you start out on a new skill, there's only one way to go – and

that's up! Of course, there will be pitfalls and disappointments along the way, which brings me to my next objection...

'I can't do it. It's too difficult!'

We seem to have this idea that writers are some kind of strange species who wander around vaguely for much of the time, being zapped periodically by something called inspiration, enabling them to effortlessly trot out Booker-prize winning novels. Unfortunately, it doesn't quite work that way. Like anything else, writing takes time, effort and patience. It's also, as an occupation, pretty isolating, and if you can't cope with staring at four walls a lot of the time, it's possibly not for you.

Okay, so there are some moments – and they are precious and wonderful – when everything seems to fall into place. There are moments, often when I least expect them, when suddenly the right words seem to come to me, out of the blue, and it really does feel as if some kind of magic has taken place. I might be lying in bed half asleep, or have just woken up, or be walking in the park, and all of a sudden, a complete poem will form in my head and I have to write it all down quickly, before it goes away.

Artists and writers often talk about their Muse in anthropomorphic terms, like a person or outside force which visits them, imparting beauty and wisdom. But if that's the case, you still need to make them welcome. When I'm not feeling particularly inspired – which is a lot of the time – I'm busy learning, training and practicing, so that when my Muse visits, I'm ready. Just as pianists practice scales, or athletes run laps round the track in the months leading up to a big race, so doing writing exercises, and reading and studying the writing of other poets, helps me improve my technique. Even when I can't write anything, just listening to poetry, and having those rhythms running in my head, prepares me for the day – rare and beautiful – when inspiration might strike. And when it does, my brain will know just what to do, because it will have become such a part of me it's almost second nature. Inspiration plus perspiration equals success.

Words are magic

So far, so good. We've established that you *are* a writer and you are an artist – regardless of whatever your inner critic might say! But the purpose of this book is not just to get you writing (though I hope it does!) but also to encourage you to use your writing as a way of listening to your inner voice.

Why do you write? You might write because you want to earn money from it (as well as writing creatively, I also work as a journalist and copywriter). You might write as a form of therapy, in order to get down feelings that you have difficulty processing any other way, or to help others going through similar emotions. Or you might like to write in order to share your thoughts, feelings and observations with loved ones and friends, perhaps to leave something behind for children or grandchildren to enjoy. All of these are perfectly valid reasons.

I was asked in an interview recently for a friend's blog (the interview is reproduced with their permission in the Appendix) why I chose to be a writer. I wrote:

"I love it! Simple as that. I sing as well, and sometimes paint, but writing has always been my overriding passion. I can't imagine not doing it. I think I'd go mad!

Words are magic! I love the sound of them, the shape of them, the way they feel on my tongue, whether spoken or sung. I love the ability of words to jump off the page into my head and hold me spellbound when I listen, to capture a moment or movement in time."

When we write, we are connecting with something deep in the universe. Words are vibrations. There is a branch of science called Cymatics which can capture sound patterns. Scientists use grains of salt or pools of water and by playing sound at different tones and pitches, they can create beautiful mandala-like shapes. Every sound has its own unique pitch and its own unique pattern. So when we speak words, we are capturing these vibrations and making them meaningful to ourselves and others. When we write words down, we capture this music and call it poetry or spin it into stories which can passed down through generations. This is how magic happens...

Mindfulness and writing

You may or may not be familiar with the practice of mindfulness. You may also be wondering what a meditative practice is doing in a book that's supposed to be about writing.

I've been writing for a long time. I've wanted to be a creative writer ever since I can remember. When I was a child, my parents had a big plastic dustbin, and I'd go and sit on the dustbin because it was warm and absorbed the heat, and I'd take my notebook and write, sometimes for hours. Other times, I'd taken myself out into the fields by the house and sit beneath the trees, writing stories or poems and carefully observing everything I saw. As I grew to adulthood and went to university, then off into the city for work, my time for writing grew less and less, until eventually I almost forgot all about my ambitions to be a writer. Even if I tried to write, the words came out stilted and wrong, and I kept telling myself I couldn't do it. It was only much, much later, after taking a series of copywriting and journalism jobs, that I rediscovered my creative voice – and part of that came through mindfulness.

Mindfulness, put simply, is the practice of paying attention in the present moment, and doing it intentionally and with non-judgement. Most people live extremely busy lives. A lot of the time we're juggling work, childcare, social commitments and a thousand other things. On top of this, we're constantly bombarded by messages, calls, texts and Tweets, all demanding our immediate attention. Did you know that we receive the equivalent of 100,000 words of new information a day[ii], via television, radio, email, messages on social media, newspapers, magazines or online? No wonder we're permanently exhausted!

Mindfulness invites us to switch off, press pause and refocus. In a mindful state, we can simply observe our thoughts, emotions and body states, without having to make immediate responses. We can simply 'be'.

For me, mindfulness has enabled me to reconnect with that small child who sat on the dustbin or under the trees, calmly absorbed in the moment. I can recall when I was little being fascinated by the ants on the doorstep. I'd sit and watch them going about their business, and sometimes I'd give them names and write stories for them. On fresh, autumn days my brother and I would sometimes get up early so we could observe the cobwebs decked like jewels with morning dew. Once, walking with my father, I remember stopping still and just listening to the sounds of the birds in the trees. All of these things are mindful, in their way.

Mindfulness, you see, is not just switching off – it's also switching *on*.

Once you switch off all the nagging demands and thoughts and distractions that don't really matter, you learn to switch back on to the things that do. You see the world in a different, more vibrant way. And that opens you up to a whole new way of being, living and creating.

CHAPTER 1: FEAR OF THE BLANK PAGE – UNLOCKING THE WRITER WITHIN

"There is geometry in the humming of the strings, there is music in the spacing of the spheres,"
– Phythagoras

'Poetry is eternal graffiti written in the heart of everyone' – Lawrence Ferlinghetti

The magic of words

Words are powerful, magical spells conjured, whether spoken, whispered, shouted or sung. In the beginning was the Word. The Biblical creation myth depicts God's breath trembling over 'Tehom' – the waters of chaos – to create life.

We are born of water, emerge from the safety of our mother's womb to an unpredictable, waiting world – our very own blank page. When we write, we breathe and shape new worlds into being.

As far back as Pythagoras, philosophers depicted the universe as living in a state of constant, vibrating energy – the harmony of the spheres.

Here's a quote from Professor Tamara Davies, a professor of astrophysics at the University of Queensland, Australia:

'The combinations of notes that sound harmonious to our ears can be derived mathematically, as their frequencies make simple ratios. The orbits of the planets also happen in simple ratios. Mars takes approximately twice as long to orbit as Earth. Turned into a musical chord that means Mars and Earth play an octave. Venus orbits three times faster than Mars, which means they play a fifth plus one octave.'[iii]

At their heart, words are pure vibration. When we hear words spoken aloud, we respond on a deep, instinctual level. Babies and even animals can detect changes in tone of voice that suggest emotions like anger, joy or fear. Words have a profound impact throughout our lives.

Perhaps you remember your parents reading you to sleep when you were little? The sensation of words weaving their spell over you, words you could curl up and hide inside, stories you could lose yourself in, creating a portal between the real world and the world of dreams. Or perhaps there were other words – bitter words, angry words, words like 'can't' and 'don't' and 'won't'. Words like 'you'll never amount to anything' or 'you're no good'. Words that, even now, have the power to wound and injure.

Be careful with your words. Words have power. Words can create or destroy.

And now you have made a conscious decision to pick up your pen and write your words into the world. The world is an empty space, a blank canvas that only you can fill. But where to start?

It starts with a blank page...

Fear of the blank page is real. It takes courage to write, to make your mark on the world. If you're anything like me, you start off in a blazing fury of excitement, ready to make the idea that has been growing and brewing in your head a living, breathing thing. And then you see the blank page. And then you freeze.

Why do we do it? What is it about facing a blank page that's so daunting? Here are a few possibilities...

'I'm scared that what I create won't be good enough'

'I don't feel I have any insights that are valuable enough to share'

'Who am I kidding? I'm not really an artist/writer'

'I'm scared of releasing powerful emotions which I might not be ready to face yet'

'I'm worried about what people might think'

'What's the point? It'll never get published anyhow'.

Stop! Stop now with the negative self-talk, and focus on the facts you know for certain, the things that are real.

The Truth:

Anything you can write is better than a blank page...

Right? Don't you think that every writer ever has at some stage had these or similar thoughts. Most writers are sensitive souls (this is partly why we write). Most will have suffered similar doubts and similar setbacks. Plus it's highly unlikely any of them sat down and rattled off a masterpiece in a single sitting.

Of course what you write is never going to sound as good as it did when it was in your head, especially in first draft. And perhaps it's not (yet) as good as Dickens/Austen/Hemingway (insert name of favourite author here). But it's a start. The more you write, the easier it will become to get the words out of your head and onto the page.

The blank page is your playground. A place to make your own. It doesn't have to be a dark and scary place. Think of it as a meeting place for the people you've yet to meet. It's a friend across a table in a café, to whom you're about to tell the funniest story you've ever heard. It's that letter to yourself you never got to write. It's your favourite picture in the gallery – the one that only you can paint.

Where do you start?

There are different modes and methods of writing, and none of them are necessarily better than any other. Some writers come to the table with a fully planned-out novel, complete with fleshed-out characters and a meticulously crafted plotline, with endless twists and turns. One of my friends plots out all his storylines on Post-Its strewn across his living room floor until he can work out the best order for events to happen. For others – myself included – a single line or an idea might be sufficient to spark off a train of thought or spontaneous act of creation. Find what works for you. Experiment with different methods, different ideas. There is no right way. The important thing is to start.

Mark-making is a primitive, essential need. One of the most important stages of development comes when a toddler is given a crayon and a blank sheet of paper for the first time. Over time, random lines join up to create identifiable forms – round blobs with stick legs at first, and then people with big round eyes and smiles and eyelashes and freckles. If we're lucky, we'll continue these acts of creativity into adulthood, but it is easy – so, so easy – to stop. Perhaps somewhere along the line somebody – a teacher or a parent or other authority figure – tells us we're not good enough, or perhaps we tell ourselves.

Perhaps 'real life' – work and family and the need to make a living and respond to emails and texts and keep continually busy – takes over and we find ourselves just too exhausted to even think about creating anything. Or we see someone who's really good at the skill we're trying to master and tell ourselves we could never be that good so it's pointless even to try. Before long, in our striving for perfection and results, we've forgotten all about how it felt in the initial rush of creativity, to make something for the sheer fun of making it, and to leave our mark on the world.

'Poetry is eternal graffiti written in the heart of everyone' said Lawrence Ferlinghetti, one of my favourite poets. I'd never really understood graffiti, not for a long time anyhow. I thought it was ugly, obscene – an unnecessary visual intrusion in a world already overly crowded with urban detritus. I would rather have neat, clean streets. And then, in 2020, came the global pandemic and lockdown. Suddenly, my creative, vibrant world receded into four walls – and such dull walls! Deprived of the creative company I craved, I sank into a depression until it was a daily struggle just to heave myself out of bed. The worst part of all was feeling like I was invisible. I realised then, perhaps for the first time, that, for me, an important part of being creative is the ability to share that creativity with other people.

When we eventually all emerged from lockdown, I ventured into some of the back alleys of my home town, in search of a suitable urban location to record a video of a poem I'd been working on, and then I saw it – a scrawl of words upon a wall. Bold. Angry. Ugly, but also beautiful in its way. And suddenly, after being invisible for the best part of a year, I understood: The need to make our mark on the world. The need to see and be seen. The need to shout out our colours against the grey. To create, to write, to sing, to dance, to shout at the top of our lungs. To say: *I exist. I was here, and I matter.* To scrawl our tag across the universe.

How to Boost Your Creativity – 10 Top Tips

1. Put on some music
It's a familiar scenario: you sit down at your desk to write and find yourself staring at a blank page for hours. You give up and go to a café instead, and suddenly the ideas come flowing from your pen. Ever wondered why? Well, the answer just might lie in the background chatter. Researchers led by Ravi Mehta at the University of Illinois asked subjects to carry out a series of creative tasks set against differing noise levels. They found that 70 decibels – a moderate level of background noise roughly equivalent to what you'd find in an average coffee shop – was ideal.[iv] If you can't afford the price of a Frappuccino, gentle music will do the job just as well.

2. Switch off technology
We spend around three quarters of our time every day receiving and processing information. With so

much 'noise' it's little wonder creative thoughts can easily get crowded out. Take some time each day to switch off everything – mobiles, computers, TVs – and simply focus on the here and now. Your brain will thank you for it.

3. Get outside
It's long been known that being out in nature stimulates a sense of wellbeing, but did you know it can also make you more creative? A 2012 study found that backpackers were 50 per cent more creative after spending four days out on the trail. They also showed improved evaluation and problem-solving skills.[v] So if you're feeling stuck for new ideas, perhaps a trip to the local park is in order.

4. Keep your desk messy
Yes, really! A University of Minnesota study found that people are more likely to arrive at creative solutions to a problem when working in slightly disorganised (rather than spotlessly tidy) environments.[vi] Great news for messy people like me – though perhaps not so much for those who have to live with us!

5. Carry a notebook
The best ideas usually arrive when we're most relaxed – which is often when we are least prepared for them. Writing is a bit like catching butterflies; you have to catch the ideas when they come, otherwise they float away. Carry a notebook and pen, or record snippets of poetry onto your mobile. Not all of them

will be usable, but the more you write, the more chances you have of finding that one idea that will. Simple!

6. Change the media
Can't write that story? Then why not sketch it? Picture refuses to be drawn? Then turn it into a poem...or a song...or a short film! Sometimes simply changing the media you're working in can help shift your creative block, opening up new ways of self-expression. Connect with other artists, visit a gallery and challenge yourself to write a short poem or haiku on each painting, or listen to a piece of classical music and see what stories it tells.

7. Try some colour magic
If you're feeling blocked, try looking at something green...or something blue. Psychological studies investigating the effects of different colours on the brain have found these two colours to be the most effective for stimulating creative thought. It's thought the reason could lie with their association with nature. Green is linked with creativity and growth[vii], whilst blue is thought to promote positive feelings such as openness, peace and tranquility.[viii]

8. Daydream
Have you ever noticed your best ideas often come to you when you're in the bath or washing the dishes? There's a reason for that. When we're engaged in simple, repetitive tasks, the rational/logical part of the brain becomes less active, enabling more

creative/intuitive thoughts to take control. So next time you're feeling 'stuck', take a break, do the dishes, go for a walk or have a shower. Just make sure you get back to your desk afterwards!

9. Exercise
'A healthy mind in a healthy body' – we all know the physical benefits of exercise, but it's good for your brain too. A study in the journal Frontiers in Human Neuroscience shows that regular exercisers perform better on tests of creativity and are better at problem-solving than those who are less physically active.[ix] Time to get those running shoes on!

10. Meditate
Dutch cognitive psychologist Matthijs Baas found that mindfulness meditation improved people's powers of observation, focus and ability to describe an event – all very useful skills for a creative writer.[x] He concluded: 'To be creative, you need to have, or be trained in, the ability to observe, notice and attend to phenomena that pass your mind's eye.'

WORKSHOP: UNLOCKING

It's there within you, this urge to create. Sometimes it's curled up tight against your ribcage like a bird, just waiting for the keys to set it free. But it's there all right, waiting to sing.

But there are so many things that prevent us from being the whole, authentic creative beings we were born to be: Others' perceived opinions, our own doubts and fears, imposter syndrome, or simple lack of time and opportunity.

Here are a few writing exercises to help get you started and conquer fear of the blank page.

EXERCISE 1: FREE WRITING

If you're feeling stuck or 'blocked' free writing is a good way to get your creative juices back flowing again. Essentially, it's a way to switch off the left-sided (rational) part of your brain and just write the first thing that comes to mind, without exercising self-judgement.

Schedule yourself a set time to write – say 10 to 15 minutes – and just write anything that comes into your head. It could be in the form of a journal, recollections, observations (see Chapter 11 on Sense Writing) or any chosen topic.

The goal of free writing is not to produce high-quality publishable work, but simply to free your mind and start writing. If you're still unsure how to start, here are a few prompts (there are many more online):

- Write down everything you can see from where you are sitting – objects, furniture, the view from your window, anything. Where have these things come from? What are their histories? What do they mean to you? What is their future?

- What things make you scared? When was the last time you were really afraid? (Or try using a different emotion – happy, in love, sad, angry, confused).
- Write a scene set in a fantasy world where everyone who dies is reincarnated and can remember each of their past lives.
- Pick a random phrase from a book or poem and use it as a first line of a story or piece of prose.
- What's your most treasured possession and why?

Just write – without judgement and without stopping, for a set time. Afterwards, you might like to go back through and see if there is anything you could use for a future piece of writing. Or you can throw it away. It's up to you.

EXERCISE 2: CREATIVE DOODLING

Like free writing – but with drawing! Sometimes, if I can't write, changing the activity to a different form of creativity can help. It doesn't matter that I'm not a great artist. It's the creative process that counts! Were you a doodler as a child? Perhaps you were one of those children that was forever being told off for doodling in the margins of your schoolbooks? If so, now is your moment of glory! Simply pick up a pencil (or pen, crayon or paints) and draw whatever comes into your head. Again, don't judge or aim for perfection. Just enjoy being creative, in the way that a child would enjoy it. Here are a few ideas if you need them to get started:

- Draw matchstick men, women and animals (channel your inner Lowry!) Don't worry about making them realistic!
- Spirals are a particular favourite of mine. Draw spirals, loops and interweaving lines.
- Take a pen for a walk around the page and see where it ends up. Draw a scribble and fill in the interweaving loops with shading, dots, or flowers.
- Turn words into pen pictures. Experiment with how they look around a page. Be experimental and draw them upside down, back to front, or mirrored. Play about with different fonts on a computer screen or draw word clouds.
- Draw your favourite place or activity. Imagine what you would most like to be doing right now and turn it into a picture. It's proven that even just imagining something we like can make us happier!

So, go! Have the guts of your conviction. Make creativity your verb. Write your words boldly and powerfully into the world, as only you know how. Create, create, create!

QUESTIONS

1. How do you feel when faced with a blank page? Excited? Nervous? Scared? All of these?
2. What stops you being creative?
3. How has your view of yourself as a writer/artist been shaped by others' comments, now or in the past?
4. How much of your fear is based on others' expectations? How much is based on your own expectations?

AFFIRMATION:

I affirm my right to call myself an artist, without fear of judgement. I embrace the blank page.

CHAPTER TWO: LISTEN WITH YOUR EYES – MINDFUL OBSERVATION

A lesson from a spider...

I was walking up the hill on the way back from school. It had been a long working day and I was tired, hot, and anxious to get home. Suddenly, my three-year-old daughter stopped dead in her tracks and pointed, excitedly: "Look, Mummy! A spider!"
"Yes, yes, I see it. Come on now, we need to get home..."
But she stood stock still, and refused to budge, adamant: *"Mummy, you're listening with your ears, but not your eyes!"*

I stopped and looked at the tree she was pointing at for the first time, and we both stood and watched, entranced and fascinated, as a spindly-legged spider spun her web before our eyes. Each miniature gossamer thread grew as we watched, creating a structure of intricate beauty, delicate, yet strong. I've no idea how much time passed. I'd already forgotten whatever it was I'd been anxious to get home for. Instead, the two of us stood transfixed, enjoying this special moment together – listening with our eyes.

Mindfulness, at its very simplest, is a simple choice to live life in the moment. Approaching situations mindfully, we can momentarily forget our cares and anxieties and enjoy and appreciate the here and now. A lot of the time we do things without really being conscious of them at all. For instance, how many times have you eaten an entire meal and not really tasted a single mouthful? Or got to the bottom of a cup of coffee without realising you'd drunk it?

We spend much of our time on autopilot – in a way, we have to, otherwise we'd get nothing done. We become expert multi-taskers. It's not unusual to find me, of an evening, simultaneously cooking a meal, sorting socks into pairs and editing an article! This is even more the case in today's multi-connected, multi-wired society. We are all instantly contactable at the click of a button, even in the privacy of our homes. With social media and aps such as Instagram and Facebook, there are always voices to be heard, messages to be checked and responded to, news items and personal matters demanding our immediate attention.

Being connected can be helpful, and even give us a sense of community. The problem is that unless we make a conscious effort to stop occasionally, to switch off and slow down, we risk missing out on life's richest moments.

There's an internet photo doing the rounds at the moment, a picture of tourists on board gondolas in Venice, the most beautiful city in the world. It could be the perfect picture-postcard shot, but for one small detail. Every single person in the picture is looking at the screen of their mobile phone. In their eagerness to tell the rest of the world about their amazing experience, they are missing out on the beauty and joy of the moment itself. Often, if we're honest, we're all like that. Here we all are, on this beautiful and amazing planet for, if we're lucky, 80 or so years, on the journey of our lives – and we're missing the whole show!

So why not take a moment or two today, just to listen. Listen with your ears, your eyes, your whole self. Because that's really, in essence, all that Mindfulness is. It's incredibly simple, when you think of it. But also life changing.

Going Deeper: Seeing with fresh eyes

'The greatest voyage of our lifetime is not in seeking new landscapes but in seeing with fresh eyes' – Marcel Proust.

Mindfulness means living in the present moment. Essentially, it means being aware and awake to each moment, and being aware of our feelings and emotions without judgement and with acceptance.

It's not magical. It doesn't have to be religious or spiritual (unless you want it to be). Mindfulness is simply about letting go of distractions and taking time to focus on what is happening right here and now.

You've probably experienced moments of mindfulness before without even realising it. Perhaps you've gazed at a beautiful sunset or listened to an uplifting piece of music and felt yourself transported away from your previous worries into a place of wellbeing. Or maybe you've felt yourself caught up in the flow of a creative activity and suddenly realised that hours have passed without you even noticing.

The aim of mindfulness is not to switch off the internal 'chatter' we all live with – that would be impossible! – but to practice being present and choosing to focus, rather than allowing yourself to be distracted.

One simple way of doing this is to focus on breathing, simply counting the breaths in and out, until you feel stilled and relaxed and less and less overwhelmed by the vast number of thoughts, demands and worries that come at you every day.

Engaging in a creative task, such as painting or writing, can be a mindful activity in itself. But if you're anything like me, it's very easy for negative thoughts and distractions to take control. Am I good enough? Was that last word the right one? Will anybody ever want to read this? Are my ideas original? And so on and so on until you lose your original train of thought and simply give up!

If this happens, don't get angry with yourself (anger is another distracting emotion!) Instead, put the task aside for a moment and take some time to reconnect. Do whatever it takes to lift your mood.

Get out into nature, listen to an inspiring piece of music (dance around the room if necessary!) Take a line for a walk around the page and see where it ends up. Cut some words from a newspaper and play with them until they make something interesting. Experiment, be playful and resist the urge to judge or make demands on yourself. Just be – and enjoy.

The Psychological Benefits of Mindful Writing

Mindful writing, also known as expressive writing, is a healing way of processing your thoughts. Unlike writing with the aim of publication, mindful writing is all about freedom of expression. Instead of worrying about producing your best work, just relax and write whatever comes into your head (you can always go tidy it up later) and enjoy the freedom it brings.

Remember when you were a child and played make-believe with your friends? Telling stories is a natural part of all human experience – and it can still be a part of yours. A regular mindful writing practice can help you slow down, breathe, and focus on your thoughts and feelings. It gives you the space and permission to process emotions, so you can re-enter the world refreshed and at one with yourself.
There are proven psychological benefits of mindful writing. Some of these include:

Clearer thoughts
Writing helps clarify thoughts and understand how you're feeling. It enables you to be 'in the moment'

and focus, free from everyday distractions. Writing things down can also improve our ability to retain information, stay engaged and grasp new concepts.[xi] Unlike simply thinking about something, the physical act of writing helps put a voice to your emotions – as if you were chatting to a trusted friend.

Improved attention span
Research shows the average attention span has shrunk to around 47 seconds.[xii] Scrolling through sites like TikTok and Instagram, with their two-minute soundbites of video, probably doesn't help! Writing, like reading, is great for retraining our brains. When you write, you force your brain to focus on a single activity for a set period of time. At the same time, you're multitasking, thinking ahead to the next sentence whilst composing the current one.

Greater empathy
Writing, especially fiction, helps us see things from different people's perspective. Like imaginative play, fiction writing lets you 'try out' different situations in a safe environment and look at things from different viewpoints. This helps create greater empathy.

Better self-esteem
Writing helps you better understand yourself. Through writing, you can express fear of criticism, and mindful writing can help work through feelings of inferiority or fear of not being good enough. And the best thing is that the more you do, the better your writing will become!

Expressing feelings

Writing helps us deal with difficult emotions in a safe, controlled environment. It can even have physical benefits. In a study by psychologist James Pennebaker, participants were asked to write for a set time about a stressful incident and record all their feelings about that time. Researchers found that, over time, those who took part in the writing exercises experienced fewer stress-related physical problems such as migraines and tummy aches than those who did not.[xiii]

Creative thinking

The very act of writing can help you think more creatively. Freewriting exercises your creative muscles and lets you experiment with new ideas, freed from fear of judgement or perfectionism. Simply by letting your ideas and thoughts flow onto the page, you will find yourself becoming more playful and innovative. You'll start to enjoy yourself, too!

Write it out

Mindful writing is a cathartic practice, which can help you slow down, breathe, make sense of events, and process your emotions.

James W Pennebaker, a psychological professor at the University of Texas at Austin suggests thinking about this type of writing is 'a life-course correction'.

Instead of bottling up my feelings and emotions, writing them down onto the page helps me face and deal with the things I've been trying to avoid.

In doing so, I can learn to understand better. If I choose to share what I've written with others, I can help them deal with these things too.

How to Practice Mindful Writing

1. If you can, set aside a regular time each day, or the same time several days a week. Allocate however much time you're comfortable with – it could be as little as 10 to 15 minutes or up to 45 minutes. Allow sufficient time to settle in beforehand and to unwind afterwards.
2. Find a quiet spot, free from distractions. Switch off all technology and notifications. If indoors, declutter your workspace and perhaps include a few details to make it feel attractive or personal things such as pictures or posters which inspire you.
3. You can choose to set a theme each time, such as a memory, writing about an object, sense writing, journaling, a gratitude journal, or simply write every thought that comes into your mind for a set period of time.
4. Before you start to write, allow yourself some time to settle into the moment. Close your eyes. Take a few deep breaths, gently in and out. Be aware of any physical sensations,

sounds, or movement. Be aware of each part of your body in turn, starting with your head and neck, all the way down to your feet and toes. Gently relax any muscles which feel strained or tense. When you feel you have reached a sense of calm, open your eyes and be aware of your surroundings again. You are now ready to write.

5. For a set time, write out your thoughts. If you find yourself becoming distracted, or other thoughts arising in your mind, gently bring your attention back to the writing. Focus on the here and now. Don't worry about spelling, grammar or making sense. The aim is to get your thoughts and feelings out onto the page. Try not to alter or edit as you go.

6. Afterwards, spend some time processing any thoughts or emotions that have arisen during your time writing. Reread what you have written. What situations did you write about? How did it make you feel? Are there thoughts or emotions that you had not expected? Do you feel you have learned from the experience, or has it changed your viewpoint in any way?

7. Allow yourself to settle for a while afterwards, before rushing back into everyday tasks. If you have dealt with difficult things, perhaps spend some time writing five things you are grateful for, to offset any negative feelings. Gently let yourself rise and return.

Small Is Beautiful – Mindful Micropoetry.

'I am a camera with its shutter open, quite passive, recording, not thinking' – Christopher Isherwood.

One way to practice Mindful Writing is through micropoetry. Micropoetry is a generic term which covers forms of poetry which are intentionally short and focus on small, precise details.

A micropoem is like a photograph or a painted miniature which captures the essence of a scene or object concisely, and with beauty. Some examples of micropoetry are:

Imagism
Imagism was a poetry movement or style of poetry started by Ezra Pound, around the period of 1914-1930, and participated in by other poets including Hilda Doolittle, John Gould Fletcher, Amy Lowell, Richard Adlington, FS Flint and DH Lawrence.

It was a reaction against the florid, elaborate and highly structured poetry that was popular at the time. Instead, imagist poems were simple and immediate, capturing a moment in time.

William Carlos Williams, in 1908, wrote of his 'ultimate aims of poetry' as:

- To paint the thing as I see it
- Beauty
- Freedom from didacticism

- Originality (so far as possible).[xiv]

Imagist poems were observational. There were no similes or symbols, no moralising or politics or striving for the spiritual. They were clearly written, with no fixed meter or rhythmical form. However, they aimed to capture musicality and beauty. A famous example is the two lines of Ezra Pound's 'In A Station of the Metro':

'The apparition of these faces in the crowd,
Petals on a wet, black bough'.

Haikus
The haiku first emerged in Japanese literature in the 17th century.

Haikus focus on a brief moment in time, juxtaposing two images and creating a sudden sense of enlightenment.

Traditionally, a haiku has three lines. The first and third line contain five syllables and the second line has seven syllables. A haiku does not rhyme. (Modern haiku often don't follow the strict 5-7-5 syllable structure). Traditionally, haikus deal with natural subjects and the seasons.

Tanka
A tanka is a related form to haiku. In English, the syllable structure is:
1st line – 5
2nd line – 7

3rd line – 5
4th line – 7
5th line – 7

A tanka can be about any subject, but often follows similar themes to haiku. Because it is slightly longer, there's more room for developing a theme.

Lune
A literary professor named Robert Kelly invented the lune, a 13-syllable poem, divided five/three/five. He named it the lune because, when written down, the right side of the poem resembles a crescent moon. For example:

Shining above me
Brittle moon
Sharp as a nail slice

Tan(g)ka
A new form of poetry, invented by Danny Gallardo of the Tan(g)ka Poetry Group. There is no rhyming or meter structure. Instead of syllables, the poem is structured by number of words, with the first line being one word, the second line being two words, and so on.

The complete Tan(g)ka poem is structured as follows:

Verse 1
1st line – 1 word
2nd line – 2 words

3rd line – 3 words
4th line – 4 words
5th line – 5 words

Verse 2
1st line – 5 words
2nd line – 4 words
3rd line – 3 words
4th line – 2 words
5th line – 1 word

Tan(g)ka are easy to write because you don't need to worry about syllables, rhyme or meter. They are also fun to read, because the structure creates an interesting feeling of progression.

WRITING EXERCISE: MICROPOETRY

Experiment this week with writing micropoetry. Don't worry too much about structure and form. Just concentrate on getting down three or four lines that capture the essence of a moment or object.

Once you're feeling bolder, you might try experimenting with haikus, tankas and some of the other forms given above.

QUESTIONS:

1. How helpful was the Mindful Writing exercise?
2. What thoughts/ideas came up as a result? Were they pleasant/unpleasant?

3. How can you incorporate mindfulness into your regular writing practice?
4. How does micropoetry help you see and appreciate the world around you?

AFFIRMATION:

**I grant myself permission to take time out.
To simply Be.**

CHAPTER THREE: THE SEEDS OF CREATIVITY – WHERE DOES CREATIVITY COME FROM?

'Creativity is seeing what others see and thinking what no-one else has thought.' – Albert Einstein

'You can't use up creativity. The more you use, the more you have.' – Maya Angelou

'Creativity is nothing but a mind set free' – Torrie T. Asai

What is creativity and why do we create? For me, creativity is something I have to do – essential to my survival. Every day my mind processes so many thoughts and feelings it's like a huge over-stuffed handbag. I have to clear it out, find somewhere to put all that stuff, to sort it out into categories, in order to function.

The writer Pearl S Buck puts it like this:

'The truly creative mind in any field is no more than this: a human creature but abnormally, inhumanly sensitive. To him...a touch is a blow, a sound is a noise, a misfortune is a tragedy, a joy is an ecstasy, a friend is a lover, a lover is a god, and failure is death. Add to this cruelly delicate organism the overpowering necessity to create create create – so that without the creating of music or poetry or books or buildings or something of meaning, his very breath

is cut off from him. He must create, must pour out creation. By some strange, unknown, inward urgency he is not really alive unless he is creating.'[xv]

For me, the medium of creating is less important than the act of creativity itself. If I can't write, I sing or play music, or make art. If I can't do any of those things I get out into nature and appreciate the creativity of the natural world – or listen to music, or read poetry, or absorb myself in books or visit galleries. I need creativity – mine or others' – in order to function.

I don't think I'm alone. I think creativity is a human need. In fact, it might be argued that being creative is what *makes* us human. Other animals, of course, do create things, and some can appear extremely artistic, Male bowerbirds, for example, create extremely elaborate nest-like structures using shells, twigs and brightly-coloured objects and will meticulously arrange them by size and colour to create the most attractive 'artwork'. The Pufferfish mating ritual includes creating large, geometric sand circles to attract a mate, which look like underwater crop circles.

But all of these things are done for a reason – to attract a mate, or to build a home, or to give themselves an evolutionary edge over their competition. Now, it might be argued that some forms of creativity do help attract the opposite sex (I mean, rock groups attract groupies for a reason!) But

– and this is an important but – it seems to be a uniquely human trait *to want to create simply for the pure pleasure of creating.*

Creativity, of course, can encompass many different things. For instance, it might include:

- Coming up with new and innovative ideas
- Physically creating something – art, music, dance, writing, building
- Lateral thinking – thinking innovatively or 'outside the box'.

Creativity is **all** these things, and more…

"To be creative means to be in love with life. You can be creative only if you love life enough that you want to enhance its beauty, you want to bring a little more music to it, a little more poetry to it, a little more dance to it." — Osho

"When you make music or write or create, it's really your job to have mind-blowing, irresponsible, condomless sex with whatever idea it is you're writing about at the time. " — Lady Gaga

Creativity involves imagination. It is personal yet somehow also universal. To be creative, we must first learn specific skills, but then we learn how to break them. There's something about creativity that is inherently chaotic, irrational, passionate, radical, anarchic. We seek inspiration, but it often seems to come to us when it is least unexpected.

So can it ever really be pinned down, analysed, or understood? Is it pointless even to try?

The Psychology of Creativity – or what's *really* going on inside your head when you write?

Scenario 1:
I'd been struggling for weeks to try to remember a tune I was trying to learn on the hammer dulcimer. Every time I tried, I could get as far as the middle section but after that, no matter how many times I'd listened to the tune beforehand, my brain just couldn't recall the following notes. I'd tried every possible way of remembering: listening to the tune again and again, rehearsing the patterns with my hands. Nothing worked. Eventually, utterly frustrated and tired, I went to bed.

After sleeping for an hour, I was suddenly wide awake. I got up out of bed, went over to the instrument, picked up the hammers and played the full piece straight through, note perfect, without even thinking. What had happened in the time between going to sleep and waking?

Scenario 2:
'A magazine I loved was asking for pieces about the Sea. I'd done all the right things. I'd spent days and weeks researching myths and folklore of the sea, symbolism of the sea and water, famous poems and stories about the sea. I'd visited the beach where I'd

stood and listened to the rhythms of the waves, absorbing the energy, in the hope that it would somehow inspire me. But when it came to putting pen to paper...nothing. Just a jumble of images in my head, which refused to coalesce into anything coherent. I couldn't make sense of anything. I gave up, blaming overwork, tiredness and stress – but the reality was, my brain just wasn't co-operating with me. Then, exactly one month later, well beyond deadline, I was sitting at my desk and the ideas suddenly started flowing freely. I finally wrote the piece that had been brewing in my head – even though it was far too late to submit it. Thanks, brain!

Scenario 3:
I woke at four in the morning, convinced I had discovered the answer to the meaning of life. In a semi-asleep state, I wrote it down excitedly in my notebook, and went back to sleep. The next morning, I woke early, anxious to see what I had written. I rushed to my notebook and there discovered the words: 'Aquatic chocolate'. What does it mean? I guess I'll never know!

Where do words come from?

Creativity has always had something of a mystical air about it. We speak of creative people as 'gifted' or 'inspired' – as though words flow effortlessly from their pen from some hidden source, and all they need to do is somehow channel it and get it down on paper. It's true that sometimes, on a good day, it can feel like that. The ideas flow, we write them down. It feels effortless, almost magical.

But for much more of the time, the creative process feels like labour. We might start off with a great idea but quickly get bogged down in the details and lose the thread. Or we create what feels like a fantastic first draft but on second reading wonder what on earth made us think it was ever a good idea.

In fact, most creativity is a mix of intuitive inspiration and good old-fashioned hard work. To use a painting metaphor, the skill of the artist is in choosing the correct colours, composition and lines, but it's that added 'x-factor' – the skill of an inspired creator – that gives the painting its edge of originality and artistry.

How many times have you sat and listened entranced to a favourite piece of music? On one level, you could analyse the skills and techniques of its composer – the way, for example, certain notes harmonise, or the way the listener is tricked into expecting one thing and suddenly the piece delivers another – a major chord that suddenly sweeps to minor. This is the skill – the 'tricks of the trade' if you like. But beyond that, in a really good piece of music, there's something else you can't quite put a finger on – something about it that hits you in a way you can't explain, like the high note Mariah Carey hits on her recording of 'O Holy Night' at the very end, which moves me to tears every single time. Skills plus inspiration.

In psychology terms, whenever we participate in a creative activity, we are engaging three networks of our brain. These are:

- The **Default Network** – the brain's inactive mode
- The **Executive Network** – the decision and emotion centre
- The **Salience Network** – determines what things you will always notice and what things you don't.

The default network generates ideas, the executive control network evaluates them, and the salience network decides which ideas get used.

So, when we create something, we are using both the rational, logical part of our brain (the part which controls decision-making) and also the more intuitive 'inactive' part.

Creativity normally starts with an initial idea – perhaps a concept, a word or a phrase, or a line of music, on which we can build. This is intuitive and not yet fully developed.

Next comes the 'collecting' phase. This is where the logical brain is engaged in gathering information and material, in preparation for the final piece.

Then comes the actual process of 'making' – the composition of music, words, paint or whatever else we choose. This is a mix of all three networks. We create intuitively. But all the time, we're making decisions – some of them sub-conscious – about what to include, what to leave out, how best to structure the composition.

Next comes the hard labour – the editing, redrafting, working up initial sketches using all the skills we've learned over years and years of practice, until we finally have produced something we're proud of.

Of course, not every single composition works exactly like this. If you're lucky and the ideas are flowing, you can sometimes skip the 'rational' parts altogether and produce the whole thing in one blinding flash of inspiration. But normally, it will be a combination of intuitive and logical thought.

The value of the creative pause

Have you ever wondered why some of the best ideas always seem to come when you least expect them – when you're in the shower, dozing off to sleep, or going for a walk in the park?

It turns out, there might be a scientific reason for this. In fact, psychologists have termed it 'the shower effect'.[xvi] Essentially, when you relax, your brain goes from a busy 'alpha' to creative 'betawave' state. In this state – which is similar to what happens when people meditate – the 'rational', decision-making part of the brain is switched off, allowing more intuitive thoughts to take over. It's the equivalent to switching off the 'red editing pen' part of your brain. Imagine your brain as being like a dog which is let off the leash and able to run around freely and unconstrained.

So if you're feeling creatively blocked, instead of agonising over your next paragraph or beating yourself up about the massive hole in your plot, a relaxing shower might be just what's needed!

CREATIVE APPROACHES

The psychologist Margaret A Boden in her article 'Creativity as a Neuroscientific Mystery' [xvii] suggested there are three different creative approaches people use:

Combinational Creativity

This type of creativity collects together as much information as possible on a subject, and then uses this to trigger new ideas. The best way for this to work is to research first, let the ideas incubate, and then engage in a relaxing activity, letting your mind flow freely without being critical.

Example: You are asked to write a piece about birds. You research everything you can about birds, their habits, symbolism, use in folklore, collective terms for birds, their physiology. After noting down your ideas, you rest or take a short walk. Later on, you are struck with an idea of the perfect way to frame your piece of writing.

Exploratory Creativity
This method involves exploring beyond what you know, experimenting and being curious.

Example: Okay, everybody knows that birds play a big role in the folklore of certain nations, but one ceremony in particular catches your eye, and you're curious to know where it came from. So you do a bit of digging and there are certain similarities to a fairytale you read about years ago and you wonder if there might be a link between them so you do a bit more digging and...off you go.

Transformational Creativity
This is thinking 'outside of the box' or thinking the impossible possible. It's the sort of maverick thinking used by a scientist who challenges known 'facts' about a subject and says 'what if this were possible instead?' Or the sort of poet who writes sentences down, cuts them to pieces, puts the words in a paper bag, shakes them up and sees where they fall.

Example: So everyone knows that birds fly, make nests and sing. But let's imagine they didn't. How would they function? What if a person did these things instead? What if we've got it wrong about birds all along and they weren't cute, friendly creatures but an evil force out to get us? (Alfred

Hitchcock's The Birds) What is there were no such things as birds? What if birds ran the world and kept people in cages?

And finally...

Creativity is a verb...

"The word 'create' is a verb. It's an action. Creativity is best thought of in the same way. It's something you can use while involved in an activity, like painting, writing, debating or dancing" – Scott Berkun.

Creativity takes guts...

'And by the way, everything is writeable about if you have the outgoing guts to do it, and the imagination to improvise.' – Sylvia Plath.

- *'Creativity takes courage.'* — Henri Matisse
- *'Learn the rules like a pro, so you can break them like an artist.'* — Pablo Picasso

The Cycle of Creativity

'In Art, the Trinity is expressed in the Creative Idea, the Creative Energy, and the Creative Power – the first imagining the work, then the making incarnate of the work, and third the meaning of the work' – Dorothy L. Sayers, The Mind of The Maker.

Whenever we create anything, be it a poem, a novel, an artwork or a song, the process of creation follows a similar pattern:

Stage One: Conception

Everything starts with an initial idea. The idea is eternal, timeless. In the idea, we see the whole world complete at once, the end in the beginning. This is the moment of inspiration. Before we put pen to paper, the Idea is already living and breathing, and starting to grow.

This is the moment of inspiration. An idea seizes you and you become captivated by its potential. You're excited, so excited you can barely think of anything else. You can't eat or sleep or think properly until it is done. In your head it's already fully formed. You feel enthralled, excited, breathless by all the latent potential. Feeling inspired is like falling in love or perhaps – to use another creative metaphor – a bit like sex. An idea is conceived and starts to take form.

Stage Two: Labour and Birth

Once the idea has been conceived, the process of creation begins. Like a baby growing in the womb, the idea becomes incarnate, it grows legs, a head, a brain. Next comes the reality, the act of creation. The hard labour. The work. The painting, the writing, the editing, the endless drafts, redrafts, proofs, reproofs and corrections. If I'm lucky I'm able to push through the pain, but there are moments, many moments, when I ask myself how I got myself into this mess in the first place and if it's ever worth it. I vow never, ever to put myself through this again. And then, finally, my new creation is birthed into the world, and it is wonderful, it is exciting and, even though it's never anything at all like I initially imagined it would be at the first moment of conception, I love it with all my tiny beating heart. And then...

Stage Three: Leaving Home

The process of creation doesn't stop with the artwork being born. Now our creativity is out in the world, it starts to take on a life of its own. You'd think this would be the easy part, but my experience is that it often triggers a kind of existential crisis. In my hands, I am holding my shiny new book. It is everything I ever dreamed of. So why am I suddenly feeling waves of fear, imposter syndrome (that old friend again!), even something that feels a little like grief? The reason is that the process of creation isn't yet finished. The creation I've birthed into the world needs to go and do its job – independent of me. A song is nothing until it is sung. Music not listened to is just notes on a page or in my head. A book is nothing until it has been read.

The final act of creativity comes at a cost. We have to risk letting our ideas make their own way in the world. I have to let go – to accept that it's no longer just mine. I also have to risk others' reactions, both good and bad.

We often think of creativity as a linear process, but it isn't – it's a cycle. We create something which goes on hopefully to inspire others. Once it leaves us, it takes on a creative life of its own.

A word is never entirely spoken, but latent in everything it touches. Our words inspire new words into the world. An endless spiral of creativity.

QUESTIONS:

1. What is your preferred form of creativity?
2. How well do you relate to the idea of the three different stages of creativity – conception, birth, and leaving home?
3. What things drive your creativity?
4. Where are you at your most creative? Indoors? When? Morning, noon or night?

AFFIRMATION: **I am part of a powerful cycle of creativity and inspiration.**

CHAPTER FOUR: INSPIRATION OR PERSPIRATION?

'Don't wait for inspiration. It comes while working' – Henri Matisse

One of my favourite commentaries about writing is the poem 'So you want to be a writer?' by Charles Bukowski. It contains some fantastic lines, but some of my favourite verses are these:

*'If it doesn't come bursting out of you
in spite of everything,
don't do it.
unless it comes unasked out of your
heart and your mind and your mouth
and your gut,
don't do it...'*

*'...unless it comes out of
your soul like a rocket,
unless being still would
drive you to madness or
suicide or murder,
don't do it.
unless the sun inside you is
burning your gut,
don't do it.'*

Reading this poem aloud always provokes debate. To what extent can it be said that writing is all about seizing that moment of great inspiration and running with it? Obviously, there *are* those moments – those sudden flashes when the Muse (or whatever it is) seizes you and grabs you and you write, paint, compose or otherwise create in a blind whirling fury of inspiration. But it's not all like that. In my experience, a lot of is hard slog. If I sat around waiting for inspiration to strike before writing a word, I don't think I would get around to writing very much! Apart from anything else, the sheer pressure of feeling like every word I wrote was 'inspired' would be enough to paralyse my pen for life.

Thomas Edison, inventor of the lightbulb, famously said that 'genius is one per cent inspiration and 99 per cent perspiration'. We writers would probably like to think of ourselves lying back on a chaise longue waiting for the Muse to strike whilst we spout witty monologues, but unfortunately the reality is just not like that.

Perhaps it's one of the reasons we've developed the myth – if that's what it is – of the 'tortured artist' (of which Dylan Thomas, my literary hero is, of course, a prime example). The star who burns bright, but ultimately can't contain their own genius and ends up burning out. But even this is a myth. In 'Portrait of A Friend', the biography of Dylan Thomas I've recently been reading[xviii], Dylan's friend and fellow poet Vernon Watkins describes his behaviour and public persona as a 'mask':

'His infectious humour deceived everyone but himself.

His method was not to retreat from the mask but to advance beyond it and in that exaggeration remain completely himself. He agreed readily with his detractors and did not in the least mind being misunderstood. Then, in the private dark, his exuberance was subjected to the strictest control."

And there's the rub. Genius – if that's what you wish to call it – is all very well, but it can't be sustained indefinitely. At the end, there is always the need to control. Dylan Thomas, it is well-attested, could write one hundred or more drafts of the same poem, often spending a day pondering over a single word before he was entirely happy with it. Inspiration – yes. Perspiration – most definitely.

As someone who aspires to write, the way I look at it is, I have to put in the miles, to learn the craft before it can become second nature enough to flow. I do a lot of writing exercises, I write an unbelievable number of terrible first drafts, I read and read and read until the rhythms of poetry become hammered into my brain. But then when it happens for real, when inspiration strikes, my brain knows what to do, instinctively. I don't have to think; it just happens because it has to, and that's when the good stuff writes itself.

This happens pretty rarely, to be honest, but when it does, it's the greatest adrenaline high in the world. You look at the thing you've just written. You think: 'Where the heck did that come from?' Or you'll be midway through writing a ponderous piece of prose when suddenly something takes over and it starts writing itself. Fifty or a hundred or two hundred and a thousand words later, you put down your pen.

Even then, the work isn't finished. Because once you have your first draft, there's still always work to be done. Sometimes my poems come to me in a stream of consciousness that I barely have to alter. Other times, they're left on one side to come back to, often months or even years later. Sometimes, particularly for prose, I write multiple drafts. There's no rulebook.

But the important thing is that I regularly show up. Every day I write something. As a good writer friend once said, it's not rocket science. The more you write, the more chances you have, even by fluke, of producing something good. It's the monkeys producing Shakespeare principle. Sort of.

I think what's most useful in the Bukowski poem, though, is the implication about false motives. What am I really writing for? I'm talking about my poetry here. I've written paid journalistic pieces, and the process there is very different. It's still creative, but much more ordered. You're given a brief, you do the research, you write it up, you get paid. But creative writing is a whole different thing. There's no brief, as such, though you can create one. If you're lucky, you might make money out of it (or at least cover costs), but unless you're the next JK Rowling, that's absolutely not guaranteed. From my experience, if I set out to write Great Poetry, that's when I produce my very worst doggerel. It can't be forced. It has to grow, organically.

I think if I was writing for money or fame or any of those things, I'd have given up long ago. The fact is I write because I can't help it. I'm an addict. I consume words and stories wherever I go, like a hungry worm. I write things in notepads, little phrases or word pictures or conversations or mini scenarios that have caught my eye. The idea of not writing, or not creating, is as alien as not breathing. It's just impossible. If I tried it, I'd be dead.

Another of my favourite quotes is from Rumi:

'In your light I learn how to love. In your beauty, how to make poems. You dance inside my chest where no-one sees you, but sometimes I do, and that sight becomes this art.'

I think this is closer to my own experience. It's the act of falling in love with beauty and words that provokes me to creativity.

It can't be forced, or taught – though the craft of perfecting how you put the words together can be learned. But ultimately, that 'spark', the one that's dancing inside our chests – that's something that's available to all.

Writers, dancers and dreamers...

If history is written by the victors, then fiction — that shapes the inner realities of people — is created by writers.

We are the misfits, the dreamers who got told off for looking out of windows when they should have been concentrating, the rebels who dared to keep believing in fairies and monsters and ghosts long after all our friends grew up and got husbands and wives and mortgages.

We are the seers and the shamans who dare ourselves to venture into the dark places, to see through the mundane and go safely mad every day, bringing back from the dreamworld our shapes and phantoms for others' delight and entertainment, singing our spells over the bones.

We are those you ignored at school or taunted for being different, and now we wear our difference as a badge of pride because we shape your inner world, and you know it. We are powerful. We have voices. We have dreams.

We have visions that can keep you up at night, or turn you mad like us. We are tricksters, cunning folk, wise women and men. We are the whispering voices you hear in your half-sleep, when all about you is silent and the lights are out. Your dreams are our playground. We feed off living souls.

You will find us in the corners of your consciousness, watching and waiting, analysing, writing on the scraps at the edge of days. Perhaps we will put you in a story some time. Perhaps you will notice; perhaps you won't. We are the tune and you shall dance. We are writers. Fear us!

Choose your Muse

In ancient Greek religion and mythology, the Muses were the inspirational goddesses of literature, science, and the arts. The nine Muses were: Urania (astronomy), Polyhymnia (hymns), Melpomene (tragic theatre), Thalia (comedic theatre), Clio (history), Calliope (epic poetry), Euterpe (song and elegiac poetry), Terpsichore (dance), and Erato (lyrical poetry).

Throughout history, writers and artists have spoken of the source of their inspiration as their Muse. Artists typically had 'muses' – often using the term to refer to a particular person who inspired and invigorated their art. A famous example is Elizabeth (Lizzie) Sidall, the model who posed for many of the Pre-Raphaelite artists. Lizzie posed for Millais' famous Ophelia, for which she floated in a bathtub full of water during their sessions. But perhaps the artist most inspired by Lizzie was her husband Dante Gabriel Rossetti. She met Rossetti in 1849, started modelling for him, and soon enough he was mostly painting her, and stopped her from modelling for other Pre-Raphaelites.

In modern-day use, a Muse can be anything that inspires us. It might be a person, an experience, an object, a song, or just a feeling that suddenly strikes. Sometimes, I find it helpful to think of inspiration itself as a Muse who chooses to visit. When I'm feeling stuck, or creatively blocked, I ask the Muse to visit and help me out. Unfortunately, my Muse is fairly capricious, as all Muses tend to be. I figure that if I keep on asking, and keep on showing up ready, perhaps she might deign to show up once in a while – most likely, when I'm least expecting her. That's the way of it, I suppose. I'm just pathetically grateful when she does.

Writing Rituals

What is your writing practice?

A little while ago, if you'd asked me that question, I'd have stared back at you blankly. As a working mum, my writing – in fact, any creative activity – had to be sandwiched into any available pocket of time. It was usually a case of grabbing what precious seconds I could and fitting in as much creativity as I was able.

Poems and essays were written in the bath, in the early hours of the morning, while walking on the school run, or at half past five in the morning when my brain woke me up with a couple of lines of a poem or the chords of a song. These days, as my daughter hits the teen years and becomes more independent, I increasingly value the ability to set time aside specifically to write or create. I appreciate this puts me in a position of privilege. So many great ideas, stories, poems or works of art never get created, simply because the vast majority of people are too busy earning a living or living life to find the time to be able to create. But it's important that all voices get heard – not just the voices of those with leisure to write. If not, our art is only reflecting a tiny minority. The ability to write needs to be accessible to all. So one of the things I'm passionate about is helping others find the time, and the space, to write – even if it's just a paragraph a day.

I've never been a creature of habit. The bohemian in me rebels against routine and order. My house is a joyous chaotic mess of clothes, books, art, music and unplayable musical instruments. I will never be a minimalist. It's just not in my nature. Also my body clock runs differently to the rest of the world. But I've come to realise that unless I make some kind of plan, I'm likely to spend the rest of my days talking about that novel I'm planning to write, one day, and never actually starting it.

I need a writing ritual.

You'll notice that I call it a ritual, not a routine. That's deliberate. I hate the word routine. It sounds so soulless. A routine is something you do involuntarily, like getting up and going to work in an office. It sounds far too formal and businesslike. I'm not about to straitjacket myself before I even start. Besides, there's a difference.

The dictionary describes routine as 'an act or series of acts, regularly repeated in a set manner'. Ritual carries similar meaning but has spiritual or religious overtones. As well as being an act of routine, it's defined as 'a religious or solemn ceremony consisting of a series of actions performed to a prescribed order'.

A writing ritual is a set sequence of actions that you perform before you sit down to write.

For me, creativity isn't just a rational activity. Whenever I do something creative, whether it's writing or painting or music, I'm not just engaging the right side of my brain. I'm tapping into something deeper, something primordial – inspiration, the Muse or whatever else you care to call it.

When I sit down to write, I'm not just disciplining myself to sit down to work. I'm creating the right environment in which to listen, to be receptive to that inner voice that gives me my ideas.

Creating a writing ritual is not just about finding a regular time and space to work (though that's important, too). It's about slowing down and making the space to intentionally create.

Things to consider include:

- Where do you work best? At a desk? At a kitchen table? In a café? At home? Alone? Around people? In nature?
- How do you work best? In silence? With some background noise? With gentle music?
- When are you at your most productive? (This might be different to when you physically have time to create!)
- What things inspire you? Is there a picture or inspirational poem you like to look at? Do certain colours help you feel more relaxed or focused?
- How much can you (realistically) write in a day? (Some writers find having a target helpful; others find it creates too much pressure. Do what works for you).
- How can you minimise distractions?

My writing rituals work like this (but yours will be completely different!)

- I work best between 10am and 2pm.
- I always write everything longhand in a notebook and type it up later. I find writing at a screen almost impossible, as there's too much temptation to edit as I go. I refuse to let myself edit anything until the first draft is completely written.
- I choose beautiful – but not too expensive – notepads. I like to have a pen that has a good weight and is nice to hold, and the ink needs to flow freely. Handwriting is a sensuous activity. I like to feel the flow of ink on the paper.
- If I can't work at home, I take my notepad to the café, or out to the park. Being in nature or around other people often helps me write.
- I can't listen to music when I write, though it helps me paint. I believe the emotion of the music is absorbed into the painting, so if I want to create a calm-looking picture, I'll listen to calming music.
- I can't focus in a completely tidy environment, or in a complete mess. It has to be something between the two.

What works for you?

Barack Obama wrote the entire 760-page presidential memoir 'A Promised Land' on yellow legal notepaper longhand, using a pen. He said: 'I still like writing things out in longhand, finding that a computer gives even my rougher drafts too smooth a gloss and lends half-baked thoughts the mask of tidiness'.

WH Auden was a stickler for routine. He would rise shortly after 6am, make coffee, complete a crossword and then get straight to work. His mind was sharpest from 7am until 11.30am. he worked after lunch until late afternoon, stopping at 6.30 for dinner, and never went to bed later than 11pm.[xix]

Dylan Thomas would spend his mornings reading, letter-writing and doing the crossword – often with his father who lived opposite Brown's Hotel in town. Lunchtimes were for drinking (often heavily) in Brown's, the Cross House, or the Corporation Arms. From 2pm til 7pm Thomas worked in his writing shed, often completing 100 or so drafts of the same poem before he was happy with it.[xx]

My friend Rita, author of three books, rises at 5.30am, is at her desk by 6am and writes solidly until noon, after which she is free to meet up with friends, do shopping, or carry out household chores. She is in bed by 11pm each night, ready to get up early and start again.

Takeaway point:

There's no such thing as the perfect formula for writing or creating. Find what works for you, and stick to it. Take time to properly allow yourself the space to intentionally create and, if it doesn't work for you straight away, stick at it. Some days are easier than others. Just keep going, and don't give up!

WRITING EXERCISES:

Read Charles Bukowski's poem 'So You Want To Be A Writer?' (The full version is available online at www.poemhunter.com). Which of his observations do you agree with/disagree with? Have a go at writing your own 'advice to a new writer', either as prose, poetry or as a Manifesto. (You can see my poem 'Manifesto' in the Appendix).

QUESTIONS:

1. How much of your writing is inspiration? How much sheer hard work? How much a balance of the two?
2. How helpful did you find the Bukowski poem? What motivates you to keep on being creative?
3. What things, people or places inspire you most? Do you have a Muse?
4. Do you have a writing ritual? Where, when and how do you write best?
5. How helpful do the find the idea of having a Muse? Perhaps try addressing a piece of writing to your Muse.

'Inspiration exists, but it has to find you working' – Picasso.

Go into yourself. Find out the reason that commands you to write; see whether it has spread its roots into the very depths of your heart; confess to yourself whether you would have to die if you were forbidden to write.' — Rainer Maria Rilke

AFFIRMATION:
I will keep on working until inspiration finds me.

CHAPTER FIVE: WRITING IS BREATHING

'For breath is life, so if you breathe well, you will live long on earth' – Sanskrit proverb

Inspire: (verb) To fill, prompt or induce. From Old French enspirer (13c.), from Latin inspirare 'blow into, breathe upon'.

'The poem is a machine so simple and so efficient that it only has one moving part, and that made of the most insubstantial material: lightning and breath.' – Charles Olson

Breathe

Take a deep breath. Now take another. Every day, we take about 26,000 breaths, inhaling something like 14,000 litres of air. Breathing is the most fundamental part of human life, essential to our survival. Most of the time we don't even think about it. But how we feel and how we breathe are intimately connected.

Have you noticed how, when you're anxious or afraid, your breath seems to come in quick bursts? (This is particularly frustrating for me as a poet and a singer, because when you're performing, the last thing you want is to run out of breath!) At its most extreme, anxiety can even cause us to hyperventilate – when you breathe so fast you exhale more than you inhale, increasing the rate of loss of carbon dioxide. This can be very frightening, causing faintness, tingling of the fingers and toes and, if prolonged, even lead to loss of consciousness. In extreme cases, it feels like you are having a heart attack.

Deep, slow breathing, on the other hand, can be very calming. Often, if I am nervous before a performance, I like to warm up with a slow, gentle song – my favourite are lullabies – because it encourages me to breathe more deeply, which helps my whole body to relax.

Of course, the link between breathing and physiology has been known for centuries. In yoga, the breath is Prana or vital force. Yoga practice integrates focus on breath during slow movements while maintaining asanas or yoga positions. If we focus on breathing, the control of breathing shifts from brain stem / medulla oblongata to cerebral cortex (evolved part of brain).

Many religions also link breathing and breath with God or the divine spark of creation. In the Bible, God breathed into Adam in order to create him, and the Hebrew word 'Ruach'- meaning breath– was used as a term for God. In the New Testament, the word for breath, wind and spirit is the same. So when we talk of having God's spirit within us, we are actually breathing in the divine.

You might wonder why, in a book about writing, I am focusing so much on breathing? Well, writing is breathing. When I write, I am hearing the words on my head as if they are spoken. When I perform, they come to life, living all over again in the ears of those who hear them. Whether consciously or not, whenever I write, I am also taking pauses, breaths. For a poem, this might be a breath at the end of each sentence, or each phrase. If I am angry, this will likely affect the form of the poem. Likewise, if I am feeling very calm, this, too, will become a part of my poem. I can, if I choose, use these pauses for breath to spring a surprise on the reader, perhaps pausing unexpectedly at the end of a line, or serving up a different word when they were expecting a rhyme.

But I think it goes even deeper than that. The life we breathe through our poems becomes a form of dance. The American poet Charles Olson described it as a transfer of energy between writer and reader, like an electric spark a 'terrible fire' or 'lovely power'.

Perhaps a simpler way to look at it is like this: When we create poetry, or a piece of writing, we 'breathe in' all sorts of ideas, influences, and images. Perhaps we also breathe in a little of the divine, of magic, of wonder. We are 'inspired' (is it any wonder that the word 'inspire' comes from the Latin word for 'to breathe into'?)

But then, once we have breathed in, we have to breathe out again. When we breathe out our poem, it becomes a living thing again, not a fixed thing in our head, ready to be breathed in by others so that they, too, might become inspired to create something of their own. And so the cycle goes on....

Poetry – A Terrible Fire

'The head, by way of the ear to the syllable, the heart by way of the breath, to the line.' – Charles Olson.

In his manifesto *'Projective Verse'* (1950)[xxi] the American poet Charles Olson proposed a new view of poetic structure based on breath. His ideas, which were taken up by other poets including William Carlos Williams, led to a more naturalistic way of writing, for the ear, rather than the printed page. This led to a move away from more 'traditional' structures of poetry focused on rhyme and meter to more naturally flowing 'free verse' which follows the patterns of speech.

Poetry is possible, according to Olson, only when the poet reaches 'down through the workings of his own throat to that place where breath comes from, where breath has its beginnings, where drama has to come from, where, the coincidence is, all art springs.'

Reading a poem is a transfer of the 'energy' of the poet's breath and speech to the reader. He refers to it variously as being like an electric spark, a 'terrible fire' or 'lovely power.'

Breathwork

'My place is placeless, a trace of the traceless. Neither body or soul. I belong to the beloved, have seen the two worlds as one and that one call to and know, first, last, outer, inner, only that breath breathing human being' – 'Only Breath', Rumi.

Breathwork is the practice of using specific breathing techniques to improve physical, mental and emotional health. It can be used as a tool to boost creativity, as well as reduce stress and anxiety.

When you engage in intentional breathing techniques, it helps you relax and enter a 'state of flow'. This state is characterised by heightened awareness, deep focus and a sense of being 'in the zone'.

Breathwork Exercises:

Deep belly breathing
Lie somewhere safe, comfortable and still.
Inhale deeply through your nose, filling your lungs and belly with air.
Exhale slowly through your mouth, letting all the air out.
Repeat for several minutes.

Box breathing
Inhale for four seconds, hold your breath for four seconds, exhale for four seconds.

Repeat for several minutes.

Flow state

'The flute is really empty. It is the breath that flows through, sings and dances. To be empty is not emptiness' – Rumi

The term 'flow state' was first popularised by the Hungarian psychologist Mihaly Csikszentmihalyi. He defined it as: 'being completely involved in an activity for its own sake. Time falls away. Every action, movement and thought follows inevitably from the previous one, like playing jazz. Your whole being is involved'.[xxii]

Flow state happens when we become totally absorbed in an activity – be it a creative activity like writing or painting, a craft or sport or any other activity which requires total focus,

Suddenly, we are no longer conscious of time. We feel free, happy and in complete control of the task. The words suddenly start to write themselves.

Sounds great, doesn't it?

Unfortunately, most of our lives are the very opposite of this calm, composed state we need to be in to create our best work. We live on an ever-accelerating hamster wheel of work and domestic activities – barely able to catch our breath long enough to grab some sleep before the next day of stress begins!

Stress is one of the greatest creativity blockers. A constant state of 'fight or flight' speeds up our heart rate and breathing, in order to deliver oxygen through the body so it's pump-primed to deal with any threats. This results in less oxygen getting to the brain, making it even harder to focus or think clearly, let alone create.

Deep breathing can help slow down this stress response, put us back 'in the moment' and return to a state of calm.

Inspiration: Breathe it in

The word 'inspiration' comes from the Latin words 'inspiratus' which means 'breathe into', which itself comes from the word 'spirae', meaning 'to breathe'.

'Inspiration' comes from the same root as 'spirit' (spiritus). So, when we breathe, we are inspired, or 'in-spirited'.

Picture yourself...
Breathing in spirit/creative power
Breathing out creativity.

Creativity is breathing.
It keeps us alive.
It births life to others.

It is what we were made to do.

WORKSHOP EXERCISES:

Read a favourite poem aloud. It may be one of your own, a famous poem, or something you've read and enjoyed. Be aware of the breaths you take in and out. Pay careful attention to the pauses, rhythm and flow of the poem. Experiment with taking breaths in different places. How does this affect the sound and flow of the words? Listen to the musicality of the words. How does the sound of the words influence the way you feel when you read or hear the poem?

Taking breath as a theme, write a poem about your creative life. What do you breathe in? What do you breathe out? Think about breath as a symbol for life itself, as well as a symbol for inspiration.

Listen to some chants. If you wish, join in with some of the singing. Relax deeply into the music, breathing in and out with the chants. Notice how deeply relaxed you feel.

Experiment with writing a piece based on breathing. If it helps, you could structure it like this:

I breathe in...I breathe out...
With every breath, I...
I breathe in...I breathe out...
With every breath I release...
With every breath I bless...
I let go of...I am grateful for...

QUESTIONS:

1. How helpful do you find the idea of writing as breathing?
2. How conscious are you of your breath when reading and performing poetry or song?
3. How can deep breathing help you stay calm and refocus?

AFFIRMATION:
Writing and creativity is as natural to me as breathing.

CHAPTER SIX: DITCH THE PEBBLE IN YOUR SHOE – DOUBT AND CRITICS

' There is nothing that teaches you more than regrouping after failure and moving on. Yet most people are stricken with fear. They fear failure so much that they fail. They are too conditioned, too used to being told what to do. It begins with the family, runs through school and goes into the business world.' – Charles Bukowski

'The worst enemy to creativity is self-doubt' – Sylvia Plath.

'It isn't the mountains ahead to climb that wear you out; it's the pebble in your shoe.' – Muhammad Ali

What's holding you back?

Some time ago I took part in a ten-day writing challenge. The idea of the challenge was simple: I was sent a series of daily prompts, which I then used as a basis for writing 30 minutes a day, for ten days.

I expected the prompts to be challenging, uplifting and thought-provoking. What I didn't expect was what happened next.

A lot of the prompts were focused around the idea of creating a better vision for yourself. For the first day's challenge, we had to create inventive titles for ourselves, using descriptions that fitted what we like to do and how we liked to be seen. I enjoyed that one.

On day three, we were asked to write as if we were speaking to a younger version of ourselves. To my surprise, my 'inner child' turned out to be a disaffected teenager who was disappointed in me:

'It could've been so different,' she said, 'You had so much enthusiasm, so much potential. Where did it all go wrong?'
'I'm sorry,' I said, 'I should've listened. Real life got in the way...'
'It's not too late,' she said, 'Come here'.
She offered me her hand. I don't know why, but I took it. She walked back over to the dustbins. She sat on one, I sat on the other. Swinging our legs. Writing. 'See,' she said, 'It's not so difficult. Not once you begin...'

I turned to reply, but there was nobody next to me, only a small indent on top of the dustbin lid, where she had been sitting. Her notepad was gone too, but mine was filled with strange, unfamiliar words. I went on writing and writing. I haven't stopped.'

But the biggest surprise came on, I think, day five, the title of which was 'Breakthrough'. We were invited to write about any limiting beliefs or toxic messages we had absorbed through others which were keeping us from fulfilling our true potential. I sat down still and

silent for about fifteen minutes, let my mind drift…and then it all came flooding out.
Back when I was on maternity leave, I was made redundant. Losing my job with a young baby to support was bad enough, but the manner in which it was done was deeply humiliating. As part of the rationale for 'letting me go', my boss had put together, in my absence and with no consultation, a document assessing my abilities. Despite an unblemished track record, which included a nomination for a national journalistic award, under the column headlined 'Future Potential' were the words…13 per cent.

I challenged the decision, but got nowhere and in the end, I settled for a small redundancy payout and enjoyed the chance to spend as much time as possible with my beautiful daughter. One day, when I was at the bank negotiating an overdraft, the woman cashier asked if I worked. When I told her I'd lost my job when my baby was born, she scowled at me and said 'Oh, you'll never work again, then'. I went home in tears, feeling an abject failure.

As soon as my daughter was at school full-time, I began freelance writing and editing. I had a steady trickle of work, and I honestly thought I had put everything behind me. But when I started on the writing prompt, out it all came….

Thirteen per cent. That figure. Somehow, in the back of my mind, that total had become lodged, like a stone in my shoe I couldn't get out. So I looked at it. I took it out. I examined it some more.

I thought about how ridiculous it was that I'd carried that stone – for almost a decade – and allowed it to grow and grow and fester until it had molded itself to my sub-conscious. I had actually started to believe that I was worthless, that I would never do well again. And then I thought about how ridiculous it was. How on earth could anybody put a figure on another person's potential?! I thought about my beautiful daughter, the moment I first saw her newborn face and perfect tiny fingers and fingernails, and of all the amazing potential she held within her – a whole life's worth! I thought of how each one of us is a miracle of infinite potential. I realized that this number that had been limiting me for so long was just that – nothing but a random number on a page – and bore no resemblance to who I was as a person. And I made the conscious decision to throw it away. Since then, something rather magical has happened. I have stopped saying 'no' to projects just because I thought I wasn't worthy of them. I have stopped thinking of myself as a failure, limited by past hurts or disappointments. I have started valuing myself, and in the process, properly valuing other people (because they have unlimited potential too!) And the work has come flooding in – so much that I can barely keep on top of it!

I had heard of the power of positive attraction before, but I'd never really realised that my own self-doubt was the very thing that was holding me back. Once I had plucked that painful stone from my subconscious...I found I was able to dance!

So my message to others reading this and perhaps holding onto past hurts or feelings of disappointment or failure is this...don't let others limit your potential. Don't let others put a percentage on your abilities, because you have within you all the resources you need to do whatever you dream.

Overcoming writer's block – or, what's stopping you writing?

Have you heard the one about the writer who sat down to write a piece about how to overcome writer's block but had to give up because she couldn't think of anything to say?

I'm guessing we've all been there. One minute, the ideas are coming so thick and fast that you can barely get them all out on the paper. The next, you find yourself staring at a blank page, wondering how you even started?

The problem about so-called writer's block is that it's almost impossible to define. Some writers question whether it really exists at all? But as someone who has spent way too many hours staring at the blank pages of an existential crisis, all I can say that it's all too real to me!

I thought of writing a series of friendly bullet points about how to overcome writer's block, but it seemed, somehow, too simplistic a response to a complex problem. So here's the best I could come up with...

It's not writer's block, it's a thinker's block
One of my favourite quotes about writer's block is from John Rogers: 'You can't think yourself out of a writer's block, but you can write your way out of a thinker's block.' Writing is difficult. If it was easy everyone would be doing it. But giving up was never in my nature. We're in it for the long haul, right? Most of the time when I struggle to write, it's either because I'm tired, or lacking in confidence, or need to spend more time planning. All of these are problems that can be fixed. If all else fails, put down the pen (or iPad or mobile), take a break, have a coffee or two, or even an early night...and then start again. And again. And again, until it works.

Go easy on yourself
The thing about the creative process is that it doesn't happen all at once, or even predictably. Usually, I begin in a blaze of enthusiasm, with a great idea, start writing it down...and then it tails off. Perhaps I haven't planned far enough ahead, or maybe the critical editing part of my brain takes over. But sometimes ideas just need some more time to germinate. On a couple of occasions, it has taken me over a year to write a poem! So if it doesn't happen all at once, don't worry. Take a break, have a bath, get out into nature, feed the pigeons (for some

reason, I always find feeding pigeons inspiring) and come back to it later, once your creative seed has had a chance to take root.

Switch off your inner critic
You know the one. You're midway through writing something and all of a sudden you hear a voice inside your head telling you 'This is no good; that's rubbish; who would want to read that?' or 'Call yourself a writer? Why don't you get a proper job?' One of my favourite books, a children's book by Laurie Fisher Huck called *Magic Happens Inside of You*[xxiii] refers to our inner critic as the Yackety Yak. Every time I hear mine, I imagine a big, hairy yak spouting lots of nonsense, and the image is so funny I find it hard to take it seriously any more. I also remind myself that no author ever wrote a perfect first draft, and that even a rubbish first draft is better than writing no words at all. And I carry on.

Create a habit
I know, I know, routine and habit aren't the most exciting of things, but creating a good writing routine can help overcome those feelings of panic and not knowing how to start. A lot of writers swear by getting up at five or six in the morning and getting all your writing done before lunch. That wouldn't work for a night owl like me, so choose a routine that fits your lifestyle. I tend to write in the day. Others find time at the weekend. Pick a time and stick with it. The more you do, the better you'll get at it – and the easier and more natural it becomes.

Silence can be golden
Is your brain constantly crammed full of thoughts, worries, fears and ideas? Modern life is crazy busy! It's not unusual to find me simultaneously writing a poem, cooking the dinner and sorting the washing – all the while trying to respond to my daughter's constant demands for cheese strings, gluepots or cuddles! Our minds are stuffed to bursting. With all that going on, it's no wonder that sometimes our creative flow gets dammed out by all the debris blocking our minds! So stop...look...listen to the sounds around you. Take some time out.

If all else fails...just keep writing
It's simple, really. If you are struggling to find the right words, just write any words. Internationally acclaimed author Maya Angelou described her writing process like this: 'What I try to do is write. I may write for two weeks "The cat sat on the mat, that is that, not a rat." And it might be just the most boring and awful stuff. But I try. When I'm writing, I write. And then it's as if the muse is convinced that I'm serious and says 'Okay. Okay, I'll come.'

Imposter Syndrome – why we are all 'involuntary swindlers'

'I still have a little imposter syndrome – it doesn't go away, that feeling that you shouldn't take me seriously. What do I know? I share that with you all because we all have doubts in our abilities, about our power and what power is.' – Michelle Obama.

'(It was) the same way when I walked on the campus at Yale. I thought everybody would find out, and they'd take the Oscar back. They'd come to my house, knocking on the door, "Excuse me, we meant to give that to someone else. That was going to Meryl Streep".'
– Jodie Foster.

'You'd think "Why would anyone want to see me again in a movie? And I don't know how to act anyway. So why am I doing this?"'
– Meryl Streep.

'I have written 11 books, but each time I think, "Oh, they're going to find me out now"'.
– Maya Angelou.

I have a recurring dream – more like a nightmare, really. It's the present day and I'm working when suddenly I receive a phone call or visit from someone official informing me that, due to some administrative error, I haven't passed my university final year exams after all, and am required to retake them all...tomorrow! I awake in a state of blind panic, wondering how on earth I am going to remember any of the facts I crammed 30 years ago.

Try as I might, there's a part of me that still refuses to believe I am the holder of an Oxford University degree, even though the certificate is sitting there, framed on my wall. It must have all been a mistake.

Surely it is only a matter of time until I am found out and revealed to be the failure I always deep down believed myself to be.

No matter how successful I am in life, there's always a part of me that refuses to believe it. I would rather hold onto the image of the small, shy dreamer, who sat on dustbins scribbling away and was bullied at school for being weird, than believe in myself as a grown, successful woman. (Even typing those words pains me. As soon as I write the words 'successful' there's a nagging little voice in my head going 'Successful? You? Who are you kidding?!')

How do we define Success? No matter how successful you are, there is always someone better at doing what you do. I can spend hours working on a complicated piece of music, but as soon as I've completed it, I'm always aiming for the next one, and the next, each one more complicated than the last. I think it's part of the creative temperament, this drive for perfection, this urge to keep on moving, never to settle, never to feel Enough.

I am not alone in this. In fact, feeling like you are not Enough is so common, we have coined a term for it — Imposter Syndrome. Imposter Syndrome is the constant nagging feeling that you are not deserving of success. When you see others achieving great things, you feel like a phoney, an imposter.

It turns out that even the most famous and successful people often feel this way. In an interview, the writer Neil Gaiman recounted an incident when he attended a conference of the great and the good and got talking to an elderly gentleman, also called Neil. The older gentleman turned to him and said words to the effect of 'I just look at all these people and I think, what the heck am I doing here? They've made amazing things. I just went where I was sent.' 'Yes,' Neil Gaiman replied to Neil Armstrong, 'But you were the first man on the moon!'[xxiv]

Einstein, one of the cleverest men ever to have lived, said this: *'The exaggerated esteem in which my life work is held makes me very ill at ease. I feel compelled to think of myself as an involuntary swindler.'*

So why does it happen? Part of the reason is that we're conditioned *not* to be successful. The American author, historian and activist, Blair Imani writes:

'Calling it Imposter Syndrome hides the fact that oppressive systems teach many of us to actively suppress and hate ourselves. It's not Imposter Syndrome, it's the consequences of oppression'.

It's perhaps no surprise to learn that women tend to suffer more from imposter syndrome than men, though everyone is vulnerable. From an early age, we're encouraged not to boast – nobody likes a smarty-pants – to keep quiet, to devote our energies towards making others feel good about themselves. Children who get things right too often are picked on and called 'teacher's pet'. There's an instinctive self-protective urge to sit tight, to not draw attention to ourselves or stand out. In the workplace, coming up with innovative solutions or challenging the status quo can easily get us into trouble.

When it comes to creativity, there's an added layer of vulnerability, in sharing what we have written, painted or drawn with an audience who might not understand or like it. It takes courage to share and open ourselves up to others' judgement or criticism. So we steel ourselves for the worst and get used to expecting criticism and if somebody surprises us by saying they actually like our work, we don't know how to respond.

For years, I felt nervous of getting my poems published. What if nobody liked it? But what if they did like it and then expected me to be a 'real' poet and I couldn't meet their expectations? Ultimately, imposter syndrome is all bound up with fear of others' judgement – and our own judgement or ourselves.

So what can we do about it? Here are a few thoughts.

Stop comparing yourself
I used to feel nervous about calling myself a poet. I'd couch it with terms like 'aspiring' or 'would-be'. I was worried that if I called myself a poet, I might get

compared with 'proper' poets and be found out. Over the years, I've learned that you don't have to be famous or successful or published to qualify as a poet. If you write poetry, you are a poet. Simple as that. Yes, there will always be people better than me, and yes I will keep striving to write as well as I possibly can. But, you know what? Life isn't a competition! You don't have to be bigger or better or stronger to richer. You just have to Be. Nobody else can tell the stories you can. Nobody else has lived your life, or experienced your exact same emotions. Your voice is unique, beautiful, and deserves to be shared.

Accept praise
Are you good at receiving compliments? I'm not, or at least I never used to be. It's that social awkwardness, isn't it? As if somebody unexpectedly offered you a nice present and you don't feel worthy to accept it. Listen – it's okay for people to validate your work. It's more than okay, it's the reason why (presumably) you shared it in the first place. Imagine if your favourite writers and artists had never shared their work but kept it hidden under the bed. Would the world be a better place? It's fine, and healthy, not to expect people's praise or compliments, but it's also absolutely lovely to be recognised and appreciated. It's even nicer to pass it on. I always think of it like this: I write to please myself, first and foremost. If I can please someone else through doing it, so much the better. If I can, by doing so,

encourage others to create and share, then I've hit the jackpot in life.

Let go of past selves
Perhaps you were picked on as a child? Perhaps you never felt you fitted in with the popular kids? Maybe you had a horrible boss or partner who belittled you? It's normal to grieve for those things. It's okay to grieve for the time you lost, the person you might have been back then if things had been different. But – you're not that person now. Perhaps you made mistakes. Perhaps you feel guilty for past failures, or are reeling from rejection after rejection. These things are part of your life, and helped make you the person you are, but they do not define you. Today is a brand new page. Take up a pen. Write yourself back into your life – the life you deserve to have, the one where you get to write your own, beautiful story.

Appreciate how far you've come
If you're feeling stuck, or struggling to understand why anyone might like what you do, sometimes it can help to look back and realise how far you've travelled. Sometimes, we're so fixated on climbing this mountain – and the next, and the next – that we forget to stop and admire the view. Give yourself permission. Take stock. Breathe.

Keep it real
Sometimes the weight of others' expectations can feel like a burden. It's great to have others around you who believe in you, but it's important to keep it

real. Let go of the pressure to be the best, to compare yourself to others, or to meet some fictional future target. Instead, focus on what you can do, right now, and enjoy it.

Don't stop
Above all, don't let your feelings of imposter syndrome or fear or failure stop you from being creative. Not every day is going to be successful. Not every draft is going to be good. Keep going. Nothing you do is ever wasted. Keep putting pen to paper, day after day.

A Lesson from The Ugly Duckling

This morning, I was thinking about the children's folk tale of The Ugly Duckling. You probably know the story. A chick hatches in a duck's nest, but it is not like the other chicks. It is ugly, covered in tufty brown feathers, big and clumsy compared to the other little fluffy yellow ducklings. The other birds tease it and call it ugly. Finally, the poor, ugly little bird takes itself off to the river and hides, too sad and sorry to show its face. It sits out through the cold winter and nearly dies. One day, when the ice is just starting to thaw, a beautiful flock of white birds flies over. The sad little bird looks upward and says it wishes it was as attractive as them. The birds tell her to look at her own reflection. She looks into the water and there...is a beautiful, pure white swan.

I've always thought of The Ugly Duckling as a story of transformation. But I realised this morning I had it wrong all along. It's not a story about an ugly duckling that turns into a swan. The important part of the story is this: *she was a swan all along*. It is only when the swan perceives herself as she really is that she reaches full maturity. The baby feathers fall off and she is able to perceive the beauty that had been hers all along.

So much of our lives are wasted trying to fit into places we were never intended for, trying to be something we were never meant to be. We beat ourselves up for not being the same as the others in the nest. We are not attractive enough, not tidy enough, not clever enough or too clever, not thin enough or too thin, too fat or too awkward and gawky. We fall between the lines. We see others living neat, successful lives and compare ourselves, or others compare us, and eventually, like the young cygnet, we end up hiding ourselves and our talents away, and unless we're very careful, we freeze and a part of us can die.

But we were never meant to fit in. Comparing ourselves to others is pointless, because we are not them. That doesn't make us better or worse, just different. Ducks are excellent at being ducks. Swans are excellent at being swans. Neither is better than the other, but it is pointless trying to be what you are not.

Once you realise the person you truly are – the one who has been waiting for you inside all along – the funny, tufty little baby feathers fall off, and you can step into your power.

You are – you always have been – a swan.

Dealing with rejection: it's okay not to be okay

Me and rejection go back a long way. When I was seven years old, inspired by a feature on the news about a girl who became a best-selling children's writer, I announced to my primary school teacher Mrs Baker that I wanted to send my stories to a publisher. To her credit, rather than laugh at me, she took me seriously. Together, we made a list of publishers, made some copies of my stories (there were no emails then) and posted them off. I was so excited when I got back my replies! To my seven-year-old self it didn't matter one bit that every letter I received was a rejection. The fact that real publishers had read my writing was enough! I kept those rejection letters as a badge of honour for years. I think I still have them in my parents' attic!

As I got older, dealing with rejection became harder. Every time I received yet another letter or email informing me that, 'yes, we liked your work, but no, it's not quite right for us', I felt smaller and smaller. What if I never was a writer after all? What if I'd been kidding myself all this time?

One day, I received an email from the editor of Poetry Wales. He patiently explained that, though he liked my work, they received thousands of poetry submissions for every publication, and had only 100 pages to fill. Reframed in that context, it no longer felt like a personal failure, more a matter of logistics. There are simply not enough pages to print all the poems.

At the same time, I appreciate there is always room to improve. When I started work, my first job as a junior copywriter was to write a piece about autism. I spent several weeks researching and writing, and was really pleased with the finished article. Imagine my horror when my boss, the senior editor, sat down with me drawing red lines through practically every word I'd written. I was devastated! But he patiently went through every change, explaining why he had made it, and at the end, I had to admit, it was so much better. He had transformed my long, waffly first draft into a crystal clear piece of writing that anyone could pick up and understand. That, too, was an important learning experience. These days, whilst I can't say I relish receiving criticism, I appreciate that it can be an important part of personal and professional growth.

Whose fault is it, anyway?

When things don't go your way, do you blame yourself, other people, or external factors?

Understanding this can help develop better strategies for dealing with disappointments or rejections.

In social psychology, Attribution is the process by which people explain the causes of behaviour and events. For example:

Success:
I got my work published in my favourite literary magazine. Hooray!

Internal attribution: I achieved this because I worked really hard at it and used my skills to create a great piece of work.

External attribution: I was lucky because I was in the right place at the right time. These things are a lottery, so I can't really claim credit.

Failure:
My piece was rejected...again!

Internal attribution: I am a terrible writer. My piece is no good.

External attribution: My piece was rejected because the magazine receives far more submissions than they can possibly print.

- How does your thinking affect how well you deal with success and failure?

- How good are you at taking credit for successes?
- Do you tend to blame yourself or external factors when things go wrong?

Dealing with critical feedback

There are many reasons why we choose to create. Creativity, as we've seen, can be purely therapeutic. Mindful writing lets us process thoughts and feelings in a way that's non-judgmental, without worrying at all about what others think of it. Some may choose to share, others don't, and that's fine.

If you write creatively for any length of time, however, there's likely to come a time when you want to share your work. Doing so can help inspire and encourage others, create a sense of shared experience and give a sense of achievement. If you're more serious about your writing, you may submit it to others for critical feedback. But this comes at a price. What if they don't like it? And if they suggest improvements, how will you deal with it?

Many years ago, I was fortunate to have one of my poems selected for critique on a programme on national radio. I was really excited and honoured to think proper, professional poets would be discussing my poem! When the day came, myself and members of my writing circle assembled at the Dylan Thomas Centre in Swansea. Microphones were checked, we were briefly introduced, and then we were live on air. Then began probably the most brutal experience of my writing life!

For a grueling half an hour, live on air, my work was picked over, word by word, reassembled, analysed, criticised and critiqued. The professional poets didn't seem to understand at all why it was written, or what I'd been intending to get across. I wanted so badly to argue but was scared of being seen as pushy or defensive, so I sat still and silent until the ordeal was over. At the end, I resolved to change nothing. Not a single word.

That taught me another useful lesson. Criticism can be painful. Some criticism is helpful, but not all. It is okay to reject other people's opinions if they don't ally with my own artistic vision. These days, I am not afraid to take criticism on the chin. Mostly, I welcome it. It helps make my work better, and improves my skills as a writer. But I never lose focus of the fact that, ultimately, my voice is my own.

I will take on board comments, criticisms and critique. And then I will sharpen my metaphorical pencil – and start again.

Top tips on dealing with criticism

Practice
Like any skill, the more you do, the better you will get. It's unlikely you'll get it right first time, but if you

keep going it will get easier. Be willing to put in the work.

Be eager to learn
Do as much research as you can. Read as much as you can, in every possible style. Listen as much as you can. If you are submitting to magazines or publishers, find out what sort of work they have liked in the past. Take out subscriptions (editors will love you for this!) Join a writer's circle. Go to open mics. Immerse yourself in your chosen genre.

Listen
Nobody likes criticism, but it can help us improve. Ask leading questions. Instead of 'Did you like my book?' ask 'What did you like? What didn't you like?' How could it be improved? What could be added or removed? Be willing to change and learn.

Be gentle on yourself
If people are overly harsh or rude in their judgements, it might say more about them than about you. Consider where their comments are coming from. Is it from a genuine concern to help you improve, or are they doing it to make themselves feel superior? If someone is belittling you or devaluing your work, it's perfectly okay to ignore them. If it's coming from someone whose opinion you value, try not to take comments personally but look at your work, if you can, from the point of view of a reader or editor. Remember, it's the work they are critiquing, not you personally.

Keep going
Don't be discouraged! Learn from critique and keep making your own (unique, beautiful) voice heard. Avoid confrontation. If necessary, agree to disagree.

Remember: Critics don't always get it right!

'Can't act. Can't sing. Slightly bald. Can dance a little.'
– notes from panel following Fred Astaire's first audition for MGM.

'There is no future in guitar music.'
– Executive at Decca who rejected The Beatles.

'Playing the guitar is all very well, John, but you'll never make a living at it.'
– John Lennon's aunt.

'That boy is an illiterate and indolent member of the class. Consistently idle, ideas limited.'
– Reports by teachers of world famous storyteller and writer Roald Dahl.

Theodor Geisel was heading home to burn the manuscript of his first book, having been rejected by 27 publishers, when he bumped into an acquaintance who had a contact in publishing. Over 60 books later, Dr Seuss as he is better known, recalled: 'if I'd been going down the other side of Madison Avenue, I'd be in the dry-cleaning business today'.

When Dav Pilkey was a child, he suffered from ADHD, dyslexia and behavioural problems. He was so disruptive, his teachers made him sit in the hallway. In the second grade, he created a comic book about a superhero named Captain Underpants. His teacher ripped it up and told him he couldn't spend his life making silly books. He is now a bestselling author.

Dealing with criticism: The Mindful Pause

The Mindful Pause is a technique many people use when dealing with difficult or self-critical thoughts. It can be helpful when responding to criticism – either your own internal critique, or from someone else.

When facing a difficult situation or unhelpful thoughts, STOP!

Stop, or pause
Take a breath
Observe your body, thoughts, feeling, emotions and physical sensations.
Proceed, with more awareness.[xxv]

The Mindful Pause enables you to stop and quietly observe how you are feeling. Don't judge any emotions that arise. Simply acknowledge them and understand where they are coming from and what is causing them.

Sit quietly, and listen to your breathing. Allow yourself to simply be.

After the pause, consider which of your character strengths could help you face this challenge. Ask yourself: Who do I want to be, moving on?

Take-aways:

- You are your own worst critic
- It is okay to accept praise
- Rejection isn't (always) personal
- Critics can and do get it wrong
- Listen and be willing to learn
- Practice, practice, practice
- Know your own voice
- Make use of the Mindful Pause
- Don't give up!

'The critic has to educate the public; the artist has to educate the critic'. – Oscar Wilde.

'You're never as good as everyone tells you when you win, and you're never as bad as they say when you lose". – Lou Holtz.

QUESTIONS:

1. What messages about myself have I subconsciously absorbed from others?
2. How can I counter these messages?
3. Who do I (consciously or unconsciously) compare myself to? Why? Who has taught me to do this?
4. How good am I at dealing with criticism?

5. What specific strengths do I have?
6. What struggles have I overcome?
7. What stories do I have to tell?
8. What have I achieved so far?
9. What can I do – right now – to let go of feelings of inadequacy and embrace my strengths?

AFFIRMATION:

I am Enough. I am beautiful, powerful and unique. Nobody can tell my story as well as me.

CHAPTER SEVEN: CREATIVE PLAYFULNESS AND IMAGINATION

'The creative adult is the child who survived.' – Ursula K. Le Guin.

'We don't stop playing because we grow old; we grow old because we stop playing.' – George Bernard Shaw.

The other day, I was chatting to my friend about 'my tree'. There's a particular tree in the park that I go to whenever I need comfort. At times of particular stress, I go and sit in its branches. I feel safe up there, able to observe the world without interacting, hidden and secure and peaceful.

'That sounds great,' said my friend. 'I'd really like to meet your tree.' And that is how the two of us – two fully-grown adults – ended up sitting in the branches of a tree.

When did you last do something playful, something childish – something gratuitously silly, even?

As children, we play all the time. When my daughter was little, about six or seven, she would slip quite easily between fantasy and reality, as if the two were one and the same. Since we walked everywhere, we made up stories wherever we went. So one of the trees up our hill became the Goblin Tree and we would tell stories about the fairyfolk living in its roots. Another very overgrown tree became the Hairy Tree because its leaves, in spring, resembled untamed locks.

When I went into my daughter's primary school to deliver poetry workshops, I took branches of foliage from the local park, and shells and rocks from the beach. To inspire the children, I would ask them in small groups how these items made them feel, what they smelt like, how they felt when touched, and what they made them think of. Here are some of their very creative responses:

'The shell is like a little world you can hide in if you could make yourself very small'.

'The teasel is soft like my cat's fur'.

'The daisy is like a smile from my baby sister'.

'The pine cone is like organ pipes'.

The interesting thing is, the higher we got through the age groups, the more logical – and the less creative – their responses became. It was almost as if they were so focused on giving the 'right' (factually accurate) response, they had forgotten how to be imaginative.

As a child, I used to find it very easy to write stories. I would sit on my favourite dustbin, and the ideas would come pouring out – some of them good, some bad, some completely preposterous. They would all flood onto the paper in my terrible handwriting, faster than my brain could keep up with them.

Now I am an adult, that process is harder. No sooner do I pick up a pen than the 'red editing pen' part of by brain switches on, and I'm filled with self-doubts:

What if my idea is unoriginal and has already been done better by somebody else?

What if everybody thinks I'm completely crazy?

What is nobody ever wants to read what I write?

What if I've been fooling myself all these years and was never a 'real' writer at all?

And so on, and so on, and so on...

Somewhere along the line, we wake up aged 20 or 30 or 40 or 50 and no longer see a pine cone as a hairbrush or a church organ or a stairway to a magical kingdom but simply see a plain, old boring pinecone. That's a great pity. No. It's more than a pity. It's a tragedy.

How do we break out of this?

As a teen, I was constantly being told to 'act my age'. I failed at many of the things adults are supposed to be good at. To this day, I'm a terrible cook, rubbish at

DIY and can't drive. It's not that I'm entirely incapable of doing these things. It is mostly a matter of priorities. While others were busy honing their adult skills, I was too busy balancing on ledges, climbing trees, talking to cats, dancing in the rain, writing poems or going on the swings when no one else was looking. I'm just – it turns out – not awfully good at being an adult.

That's okay. I'm in good company. A lot of the most creative people are also the most playful. Now, I'm not saying you have to completely abandon all sense of responsibility. Bills have to be paid. Families need to be provided for. Children need to be ferried to and from school or taken to social activities. Food has to be cooked, bins emptied, floors hoovered. But in order to keep being creative, a sense of playfulness is helpful – even essential.

It's very easy for the thing you love to start to become a chore. The more successful you become, the more seriously you start to take it. It goes from being a hobby, a passion, to something you do to make a living. You pile the pressure upon yourself to do it perfectly every time – to be the best – and, unless you're careful, become frozen in your perfectionism and suffer burnout.

A quote from Nobel prize-winning scientist Richard Feynman illustrates this perfectly. In his 1985 book *Surely You're Joking, Mr. Feynman!* the physicist recounted his own case of burnout and explained what worked to cure him. At an early stage in his life, he found himself getting bored. 'Physics disgusts me a little bit now, but I used to enjoy doing physics,' he wrote. 'Why did I enjoy it? I used to play with it. I used to do whatever I felt like doing. It didn't have to do with whether it was important for the development of nuclear physics, but whether it was interesting and amusing for me to play with.'[xxvi]

He started 'playing' again – making observations and experimenting for the fun of it – and discovered what all creative people instinctively find out sooner or later. It is when we play, when we rediscover the passion and enjoyment and curiosity and sheer damn fun of the thing – that is when the real magic starts to happen.

What does it mean – to play?

'Do not grow old, no matter how long you live. Never cease to stand like children before the Great Mystery into which we are born.' – Albert Einstein.

Think back to when you were a child. Remember, if you can, a time before deadlines, before 'to-do' lists, before exams and league tables. Think back, if you are able, to long summer holidays stretched out with a book beneath the trees, or playing football in the fields, or making dens in trees.

What motivated you then? What gave you your kicks?

For children, and even among the animal kingdom (we are only trumped-up monkeys after all), play serves a useful function in learning. It lets them try things out in a safe way. Baby animals will watch their parents hunting before practicing their own skills in pouncing or play-fighting. Goats and sheep leap and jump on and off of things, to exercise their legs and learn how to run at speed from a predator. What looks like fun actually serves a useful purpose.

Children, too, will act out scenarios they see around them, putting dolls to bed, play acting or creating stories for their toys. As grown-ups, our need to play, to experiment, never really goes away. It's just that we don't get the chance very often, unless we happen to be actors or attend one of those acutely embarrassing work training days where you're asked to role play situations with your colleagues (I can actually feel my toes curling as I type that!)

As a writer, of course, I have an extra advantage. I can 'play' in my head. In my head, I can create imaginary scenarios whenever I want to. A park can become a magical kingdom, when seen through the right eyes. And yes, a pinecone is never just a pinecone. Here are a few ideas for what I think about when I hear the word 'play' (but you may wish to add your own).

Play:

- Is experimental. Like animals learning to hunt, we know that play is not the real thing. It lets us try things out and test out scenarios. Storytelling is intrinsically playful.
- Is non-goal-oriented. The only purpose of play is to have fun! (A posh term for this is 'intrinsic motivation')
- Takes its time. Play is not time limited. It has no deadline.
- Is adventurous. Play is rough and tumble. Play is jumping off ledges and climbing up trees and hoping you won't fall. Play is learning and testing the limits of your capabilities.
- Is spontaneous. You don't make plans or 'to do' lists when you're playing. You just do whatever feels right, whether it's pretending to go to the moon or painting everything you see pink.
- Learns the rules, then breaks them. Picasso, for example, spent many years learning how to draw realistically, and then many more years learning how not to. He would later say 'It took me four years to paint like Raphael, but a lifetime to paint like a child'.
- Allows for imperfections. Nobody ever questions why mud pies are not the perfect consistency, or asks whether a finger painting is the right shade or red. It just is what it is.
- Day-dreams. The best ideas happen when we're not concentrating too hard or when our minds are just out of focus. It's that fuzzy

feeling you get when you step into the bath. Gazing out of windows is good.
- Is not limited. Anything is possible when you play. You can become an astronaut and fly into space in a teapot. You can paint using grass or custard. There are no rules. None.

From this list, you can see that much of modern living encourages us to be anything but playful. A nine-to-five, goals-driven, fast-paced, competitively driven environment is the very opposite of playful and creative. So if we want to continue enjoying creativity, we need to find ways to step away from those attitudes and reclaim our playfulness in a safe and meaningly way – most of all, in a fun way! How do you do it?

Now, I'm not saying you need to go all-out, abandon your job and take up potato printing for a living (though if it floats your boat, why not?) But you can recover your sense of fun and bring some playfulness back into your creative life. Here are a few ideas...

Some ways to reawaken playfulness

Switch everything off
Technology, especially social media, is the enemy of playfulness. It's almost impossible to feel playful or do anything playfully creative when you're constantly on call. Turn off your phone (better still leave it at home), take yourself out of the house away from distractions, and sit under a tree (or even in one!) for an instant creative boost.

Daydream
Remember how you were always being told off at school for staring out the window? Turns out most of our best ideas come to us when we daydream. When you switch your brain from rational thinking mode into neutral contemplative mode, you give yourself permission to dream up new ideas, freed from the drive to edit or see instant results. And that's when the ideas start to flow!

Do things differently
Sometimes, just changing things up can reawaken your creativity. Do you normally write on a screen? Try writing in a notebook. Do you aways write in black pen? Try writing in green. Do you always paint in acrylics? Try watercolours. Change your normal routine to awaken your natural playful creativity.

Take your mind on an adventure
Remember how you used to play act as a child, making up scenarios and adventures all the time? Well, guess what? You never lost that ability. Learn to look at things differently. The park you are sitting in is a magical land, and each area is a different territory. The copse of trees is inhabited by Elves. Can you see them? The lake is the abode of the water sprites, ruled over by the Lady of the Lake, Nimue. The food hut is secretly run by werewolves in the guise of humans. This overlaying of fantasy onto the real world can create some wacky story ideas. Just be careful to switch it off at the end of the day!

Just play!
Remember when you would dance for hours round the kitchen floor, just for the fun of dancing? When you would twiddle around on the piano or guitar, making up chords and riffs just to see what they sounded like? Remember when you wrote and wrote for the sheer fun of making up adventures or playing with words? Before the era of results and competitions and targets and deadlines. Remember that? Lay down any expectations and just do what you love. Perhaps even take up a new hobby, or an old one you'd long abandoned because you didn't think you were 'good enough'. You were always good enough. Have fun!

WORKSHOP: AN EXERCISE IN PLAYFULNESS

Do you remember how it felt when you were a child and did things just for fun? Here are a few ideas to help you get playful with your creativity:

Finger painting
Dip you fingers into ink or paint. Now look at the finger marks on the paper. What shapes do they conjure up? What could they be? A dragon's scales, a rabbit's ears, a series of little people? Let your imagination run wild and see what emerges!

Blow bubbles
Simply that. Buy a pot of bubble mixture, sit in a park or somewhere beautiful, blow bubbles and watch

them. There's something really magical about bubbles, especially where the light catches them. Meditate, write poems, draw them!

Exquisite Corpse
Here is a fun one to do as a group. Exquisite Corpse is a parlour game which was played by the Surrealists, among others. It's a method of assembling a collection of unconnected words into a story or poem. Each collaborator adds a sentence or phrase in sequence.
It helps to have a basic structure. For example:
(Name) met (Name)
In (place)
He said… She said
Consequence

For example: (Father Christmas) met (the Easter Bunny) in (Tesco). He said: (Ho ho ho). She said: (Carrots are my favourite vegetable). Consequence: (They went back to the North Pole and built a snowman).

For a poem, you could try:
The (adjective) (noun) (adverb) (verb) the (adjective) (noun)

For example:

The yellow cow brightly licked the terrible teapot.

A picture variant of this is Picture Consequences. You might have played this as a child. This is where each member of the group draws pictures of parts of a person in four steps: Head, torso, legs, feet. The paper is folded after each portion so that later participants can't see earlier portions. The end result is a picture montage which is often hilarious!

If you're feeling really creative….

You could try creating a montage picture, with each person drawing a section without looking at the others, folding the paper over and then unfolding to see what you've created.

Or you could take the words created by an Exquisite Corpse game and reassemble them to create surrealist poetry. Have fun!

For inspiration: Space and Time magazine builds a community exquisite corpse monthly on their website. See https://spaceandtime.net

Cut-up Poetry

Do you have some old newspapers or magazines in the house? Why not try your hand at some cut-up poetry? Cut-up poetry is a way of creating new poetry out of old words. Simply, you cut words or sentences from different sources and reassemble them – often at random – to create an entirely new piece of writing.

Cut-up poetry goes back to the 1920s when, during a Dadaist rally, Tristan Tzara offered to create a poem on the spot by pulling words at random from a hat. It was popularised in the late 1950s and early 1960s by writer Willian S Burroughs and has since been used by many people.

Many famous writers have incorporated the Cut and Paste technique into their work, most notably TS Elliot in The Wasteland. Both David Bowie and Kurt Cobain experimented with cut-up techniques, writing their own paragraphs or poems and then cutting them up and reassembling them to create new and surprising lyrics.

Here's how to do it:

1.   Select two newspaper articles at random. Longer features work best as they tend to include more descriptive words.

2.   Skim through and underline any particular words or phrases that catch your eye. Don't think about the meaning, just choose what sounds interesting or surprising.

3.   Do this for both newspaper articles. When you have finished, either physically cut out or write down the words/phrases you've chosen.

4.   Reassemble the phrases from the two articles, in whatever order you like. This could be completely at random (drawn out of a hat) or, as I did, linking phrases which seemed to work together stylistically.

5.   Admire your new, shiny poem.

Some of my examples are given at the end.

A WORD OF WARNING: Borrowing other people's words is plagiarism! There's a very fine line between reusing a word in a different context and stealing somebody else's work. So I'd recommend doing this only for your own amusement, not for publication. It's about playing with words and having fun, remember, NOT stealing other people's words and claiming them as you own!

Alternatively, make like David Bowie and try this method instead:

1.   Think of a subject, any subject. Let's say, for the sake of argument, how to make the perfect cup of tea.
2.   Think of another unrelated subject, say how you felt in a recent relationship.
3.   Write a paragraph on each subject. Don't think too hard. You want it to be a stream of consciousness.

4.   Cut up the lines of both and reassemble in a random order.
5.   Ta da! Your very own David Bowie lyric!

Here's what happened, for example, when I combined a poem I'd previously written about the sea with a description of a friend suffering from depression:

Threnody

Blue and grey, rolling with rain,
And the darkness moved in,
Spreadeagled an invitation,
White limbs lost to a pitiless tide

Bent and twisted,
Tongued by lolling waves,
You shouted all night to keep the voices out,
An abandoned layer of bones,
Painted your arms red to feel something real

Whirlpool clouds made of steel and dust
Loom long and heavy on the other side.

NEWSPAPER CUT AND PASTE EXAMPLES:

Final Home/Love triangle
On the mudflats of the River Roach

A love triangle involving two giants,
The clear outline was produced
thanks to a drone fitted
with a specialist camera —

Clue of an adulterous relationship,
An enigmatic figure in the background,
Burgeoning romance,
Dangerously sexual feelings,
Darwin's ship
Circumnavigating
A static watch vessel.

A Load of Hot Air
I'm folding all my clothes wrong,
according to Mari Kondo,
I've consumed dubious tonics and teas —
Transformation to fluid experiments in style,
A painting made in extreme close-up.
Breathing is unconscious —
Inhale and exhale —
Staring at pale flesh with a
grim butcher's intensity,

When I'm jostled by a rushing commuter,
Carving them up in the mind's eye,
Fretted, fleshy tones and textured mottle,
bring me back to an even keel,

Silhouetted by the merciless dawn light,
Hands thrust in pockets,
The painter locks eyes with us
in the space beyond.

I Like the Stress of a City
Stark evidence of faultlines developing
Between hardline and conciliatory elements
Within the chaos,
Sending shockwaves,
Police armed with batons
Throw stones and flares, grappling.
You find your own oasis,
The white sands covered by the grey,
The catch is worthless and often dumped:
Every now and then
I fling it all up in the air
And see where it lands.

You can see how, used with care, this technique can create new and original pieces – or perhaps individual lines which can inspire a new poem.

QUESTIONS:

1. How often do you take the time to be playful?
2. Do you think you have become less playful as you got older?
3. How spontaneous are you?

4. How has this affected your creativity?
5. How did you find the 'cut and paste' task? Did it encourage you to experiment with new forms of creativity?
6. Could you create a combination of word and picture collage?
7. What can you do today to become more playful?

AFFIRMATION:

I reclaim my right to be playful. I can be creative for the sheer joy of creating.

CHAPTER EIGHT: IMAGINATION AND THE POWER OF STORYTELLING

"Imagination is everything. It is the preview of life's coming attractions."
— Albert Einstein

'Everything you can imagine is real.' – Pablo Picasso

'Only imagination is real.' – William Carlos Williams

Imagination

Everything we know about the world is only how we perceive it. Our eyes invert images. We see things as solid yet, in reality, everything is composed of atoms with more spaces between them than actual matter. Everything we see is an illusion.

What is real?

As writers and artists, we get to construct realities. We get to choose whether the hero gets his (or her) girl, whether the protagonist wins the quest, who wins or dies. In this sense, we make little gods and goddesses of ourselves. For to create worlds is to have power.

The worlds we create influence others. What we know of past, present or future is what other creators have set down before us. If I wish to, I can go back and read an eye-witness account of the destruction of the ancient city of Pompei, written by Pliny the Elder in 79AD. I can read Bronze Age accounts of the Patriarchs in the Bible, or ancient Wisdom literature. I can hear the voices of the Ancestors singing over the bones of their stories, and when I watch old films or see old TV footage, I see the ghosts of people long-dead captured in moving pictures.

Creativity can capture a moment and preserve it forever.

But it can do even more than this. It can give us worlds we don't know yet know, worlds that never existed. It can conjure parallel universes, worlds of infinite possibilities, where the impossible is possible.

It can do all this as simply as running a pen over a page or a pencil over a piece of paper.

And, think about it, what are you doing there? You are using a pencil made of carbon – crushed lifeforms from millennia ago – to create indentations on wood made from the lifeblood of ancient forests, trees which lived and breathed with energies of their own.

Those indentations create words – tiny, insignificant squiggles which have the power to convey whole worlds of ideas, knowledge and imagination. Through them, we can connect with people we will never meet, perhaps with people who have not even yet been born.

This is the magic of writing.

There is nothing so indescribably magic as a blank sheet of paper. It contains all the potential of the world. Right now, before I write upon it, it could become anything – a picture, an artwork, a book. It is the blank waters of chaos, over which we breathe. An empty canvas of limitless possibilities.

Dare you?

Dare you write upon it?

Imagination and the power of storytelling

- Stories create genuine emotions, presence (the sense of being somewhere) and behavioural responses.
- Stories are the pathway to engaging our right brain and triggering emotions.
- By engaging imagination, we become participants in the narrative.
- Stories build empathy. Like imaginative play among children, stories place us into situations where we can play out different scenarios, test our responses, and safely experience emotional reactions.
- Stories can help us deal with different situations. We can step out of our own shoes, see things differently, and increase our empathy for others.

Stories have power. We instinctively know this. As children, we sit cross-legged, spellbound as teachers become field guides, taking our imaginations to new worlds – incredible worlds that could only exist in our heads.

We use words and stories to play, to test things out. Through stories, we can safely explore situations that make us afraid, that thrill us, that entrance us. Through stories, we can become anyone we want to – a questing knight, a witch, a dragon, a princess with the world at our feet. We can play out our fantasies, we can feel real emotions – love, anger, guilt, remorse, pity, regret, joy, passion, betrayal, terror, awe – all from the safety of a bed or a comfy armchair.

Our ancestors instinctively harnessed the power of stories. Around campfires, huddled together against the shadows, they forged bonds and identities, weaving together their histories and mythologies, the tales of countless generations stretching backwards as far as anyone could remember.

Some of these stories have survived for centuries and are still familiar to us today. The classical myths of the ancient Greeks are among my favourites. They are populated by larger-than-life characters – gods and heroes who are fabulous, but flawed, who face all too human temptations, who make mistakes and all too often face awful consequences for their actions.

Throughout history, cultures have told stories as a way of expressing deeper, inexpressible truths. Stories are how we deal with the difficulties of the human condition – of birth, life, love and death, and connection with the universe. Our ancestors understood poetic and figurative language because it was all around them. You don't have to believe in a literal beetle pulling the sun across the sky to appreciate the beauty of a story explaining the wonder of the sun conquering darkness every day.

When we try to interpret myths literally we risk losing the truths behind them. It doesn't matter if there was a real Eve who ate an real apple. But the idea of human temptation and always wanting what we can't have is universal. The myths – the stories we tell about ourselves – are important. Like poetry, they attempt to express the inexpressible – our deepest desires, our guiltiest pleasures, our passions, our most deep-seated fears of loneliness, or abandonment or death. All the things that make us beautifully human.

What is your story and how will you write it?

It's easy to go through life feeling like a walk-on part in your own drama – as if somebody else wrote the story. We are so conditioned by others' expectations of who we are and how we feel we should behave that we forget a fundamental and essential fact:

We are the authors of our own story.

I have experienced vivid dreams all my life and, for a while, I suffered from nightmares. I would wake up feeling shattered, and be scared to sleep in case the nightmares returned. One particularly vivid dream I recall is seeing the streets outside my house populated by monsters, but inside the house was on fire. There was nowhere to run! Then, over the years, I taught myself to lucid dream. Lucid dreaming is the ability to realise in your dream that you are dreaming, and to control what happens in the dream. In my case, I learned that in my dreams I am able to fly. So if something bad happens in the dream, I try to fly. If I can fly, I know that it's a dream, and from then on, I have control over what happens in the dream. Sometimes, I can even make things up, just for the fun of it! I can also wake myself up. So now I have no more nightmares. I learned to lucid dream a long time ago, and then it occurred to me:

What if I could lucid live?

Imagine if you were able to control the events of your own life? Well, the truth is, to some extent you can. And it all depends on the stories you tell...

What sorts of stories are you telling yourself?

When you tell someone you're entering a writing competition, do you immediately follow it up by saying 'Of course, I'll never win!'

That is a story.

When you look at the world around you, at the inequality, the poverty, the unfairness, do you say, 'Well, that's just how the world is. It will never change.'

That is a story.

When somebody compliments you on your writing, or a piece of art, a work success, or something you're proud of, are you immediately defensive or self-deprecating, saying things like, 'Ah well, it's just luck' or 'It's not that good, really'.

That is a story.

Words have energy. Try replacing your negative stories for positive ones. Try it! Every time you find yourself about to say something like 'Oh course, I'll never win!' try replacing it with something like, 'Well, if I enter at least I've got a chance of winning' or 'You never know til you try'. Or when you're about to put someone down or diminish their achievements, try throwing down a compliment instead. Try it. See how much better it feels.

Whose stories are you absorbing?

We talk a lot about what foods we put into our mouths. Whole industries are devoted to endless diets – the no-meat diet, the protein-rich diet, the calorie-controlled diet and countless others. We think a lot less about the 'foods' we put into our minds. But it's really just as important, if not more so.

How many times have you been in a perfectly good mood and then suddenly, out of the blue, found yourself feeling uncomfortable, edgy or low? All sorts of external factors can affect our psychological wellbeing, from the music we listen to, to the quality of lighting, or negative emotions we've absorbed from others, perhaps without even really noticing.

What sorts of music do you listen to? Certain beats can affect us in different ways. Fast tempos excite us, slow tempos calm us down. Drums are used in some cultures to create a trancelike state of altered consciousness. Minor keys evoke feelings of sadness, major notes a sense of power and joy. Song lyrics are a kind of story in themselves.

What books do you read? What films do you watch? How do you relate to the characters? How do they make you feel? Do you spend hours online, or watching the news? We now spend so much of our time absorbing negative news stories and arguing online that there's even a word for it – doom-scrolling. And the dangerous thing about it is that,

that more you do it, the more the computer algorithms will direct you to more of the same content – down and down the internet rabbithole.

When I'm feeling low, and especially when I'm feeling creatively blocked, I often make a conscious decision to switch off all the negativity and replace it with positive vibes. I have certain music I turn to, to lift my mood (Mei Lin on YouTube is one) and Podcasts such as The Emerald which deal with interesting subjects in artistic ways.[xxvii] Getting out into nature always uplifts me, too, as does being around positive friends, and around animals.

I'm not saying you have to be constantly happy, and often when you're feeling low, sad or angry music can be extremely cathartic (The Levellers always works for me!) But be mindful of what you're putting into your brain. Be mindful of whose stories you choose to absorb.

Telling new stories

So now that we've spent some time thinking about the power of stories to create new realities, it's time to start creating some stories of your own. Think about what you want to convey. What emotion is strongest in your life right now? What is your story, and how will you tell it? Here are a few points to consider:

- Will you set it in the past, present, or future?
- Whose voice will you write in? Your own, or someone else's?

- Is it based on reality, or complete fantasy (the best stories are often a mixture of both)?
- Who will read it?
- Are you writing for children, teens or adults?
- How long will it be? Micro-fiction? A story? A book?
- Who are the main characters? Who is the protagonist? Who is the antagonist?
- What obstacles are they facing? What is their superpower? What is their greatest weakness?

If you're stuck for how to start, here are a few story pointers:

- My most treasured possession. What object do you most value and why?
- My earliest memory
- My greatest dilemma
- A strange encounter
- A special place
- Do places hold emotions?
- Senses – what can I see, hear, touch, smell right now?
- A disastrous dinner date
- What can you see from your window?
- What smell do you associate with childhood? (I used this one and it became the basis for my short story, Lane End).

Don't forget that poems tell stories too!

WRITING EXERCISE: THREE ELEMENTS

Here's an easy way to create a story. In a writing group, or on your own, write down a list of elements. For example:

A lost key, a disguise, a phobia, a blizzard, a surprise visit, a haunted house, a hidden door, a talking animal, poisonous toadstools, a missing necklace, Valentine's day, a lucky mistake, a long-lost relative, an ancient castle, an old battered car...

Be as imaginative as you like!

Next, put all the elements into a hat. Draw out three at random. For example:

A lost key, Valentine's Day, a talking animal.

These are the three elements you have to combine into a story.

Take turns in trying to create the wildest, wackiest stories you can, incorporating all of the random elements!

WORKSHOP EXERCISE – CREATE YOUR VISION

'Without a vision the people perish.' – Proverbs 29:18

What stories are you creating for your own life? A Vision Board acts as a creative, visual reminder of your goals, hopes and intentions. The thinking behind it is that the more focused and directed you are, and the more positively you are able to aim towards your dreams and desires, the greater chance you have of achieving them.

Here's how to do it:

1. Decide what areas you want to focus on

Think about four to six areas of your life you'd like to focus on. Mine were:

- Wellness
- Creativity
- Adventures
- Career
- Family and Friends
- Personal growth

Try to keep the category headings down to six, or at the most eight, otherwise things get too cluttered. It might be that some of these areas require more space than others, and that's okay. There are no rules. Just divide the space on your poster into the areas that matter to you. There might be others you wish to substitute. For instance, instead of Family, you might want to include relationships/romance. Or perhaps you have travel plans? DIY plans or a house move? Whatever matters to you, list it.

2. Collect your materials

You'll need a large piece of card, divided into categories, on which to list your goals and intentions.

You'll also need inspirational words, quotes and images. This is the fun part! Be as creative as you like. Gather images from newspapers, online, magazines, brochures, pamphlets, or photographs. Keep a big file of them, but at this stage don't spend too much deciding what's 'in' or 'out'. That part comes later. You'll also need glue sticks, pins and bluetac.

3. Set your space

Drawing up your Vision Board is a fun, creative and meditative exercise. Put aside some special time when you know you won't be uninterrupted. If this is impossible because you have young children (I know, I've been there!) perhaps involve them and make it a bonding activity between you, or even get them to draw up one of their own! Set the stage – turn on some calming or happy music, pray, meditate, or do whatever makes you feel uplifted and creative.

4. Let's get going!

Think about your goals, hopes and desires under each heading. They don't have to be that specific, if you really aren't sure, or even realistic. If you have an ambition that right now seems almost impossible, put it in anyway. The very act of stating your intention brings you one step closer towards achieving it.

Once you've thought about your goals, it's time to get creative. Look for quotes, pictures or anything else that illustrates your intentions. For instance, if your goal is to finally get around to writing that novel, you might choose a picture of a book, an old-fashioned typewriter or even your favourite bookshop. Other ideas may be more abstract and harder to illustrate. One of my aims, for example, under 'Wellness' was the word 'Simple'. This encompasses both my practical need to declutter my possessions, as well as spiritual decluttering and more conscious living.

As you paste the images and words onto the board, let yourself imagine how you would feel accomplishing your aims. This part is really important, because it lets your inner consciousness know that it is achievable, and you get to experience a little of the reward in advance. Every time you look at your Vision Board, you will be reminded of this feeling, and encouraged to keep going towards your goal.

5. Add some motivational words

Once you've chosen the images, think about some words to go with them. Your vision shouldn't be so much focused on 'stuff' as how you want to feel. Think of positive words that will reflect how you want to feel about life. For me, these included words such as loving, cheerful, free, fearless, strong, empowered.

6. Stand back and admire the view

It's true what they say: a picture says a thousand words. Step back and take a look at what you've created, and add any finishing touches. Hang the Vision Board in a place where it can serve as a daily encouragement. Don't forget that the purpose of a Vision Board is not to beat yourself up about the goals you've yet to achieve, but rather to serve as an encouragement. As you grow and evolve, your dreams will too, so try to think of it as a journey, not a destination.

Say thank you daily for the blessings you've received — and the blessings you hope to receive in the days and months ahead. Dream big, believe that you can achieve your dreams, and you'll be surprised what the universe has to offer!

Heddwych — The story of a painting

We are all very good at sharing stories of success. Looking at the achievements of friends, especially online, it's easier to assume that life for everybody else is one big happy adventure. So here's a story of a creative failure...and how it ended up becoming a success.

I've always enjoyed painting — not to show or exhibit or anything, but simply for fun. I like to put on gentle music and paint Celtic spirals and it feels like a meditation, as the combined effect of the music, colours and swirling patterns calm my mind and absorb my thoughts.

But this time, it was different. It was the weekend of the Wales Air Show, a huge event held annually in my home city. For me, it always comes with mixed emotions. Whilst I can admire the spectacle and the skills of the pilots, especially the stunt teams such as the Red Arrows, I find the militarism surrounding the event extremely off-putting. As a Quaker and a life-long pacifist, the idea of pointing at the sky and marveling as a bomber plane thunders past just feels plain wrong.

So, that morning, instead of my usual music, I had the sound of the Typhoon fighter jets as they thundered over our house, leaving contrails in the sky. I tried to block it out, but my frustration seemed to bleed into the paint, and nothing would work. I could feel myself growing more and more restless, as none of the colours seemed to mix properly. My attempt at creating a rainbow effect, with colours blending from one end of the spectrum through to the other, hadn't worked. Instead, the colours clashed horribly. I felt like throwing it in the bin. I decided to leave it to dry, and went off to do the washing up, intending to throw it out later.

When I got back, the colours had dried and blended a little, but it still looked horrid. The pinks and reds clashed violently with the greens and blues, and it all looked amateurish and, well, angry. But I couldn't bring myself to throw it away, not after all the effort I had put into the initial drawing. So instead, I decided to experiment. I closed the windows, switched on some gentle music, and let the rhythms wash over me for a little while. Then I took out some metallic silver, bronze and gold, and got to work, washing over the tops of the offending colours, and re-blending them. And the gentle music and the shimmering paints worked some magic.

The resulting picture was very different to my original intended rainbow design, but still had its own unique form of beauty. It was more beautiful still, to me, because I knew it had evolved from a place of anger to a place of beauty and calm. I think there is an edge of resilience to it, beneath the layers of gold and silver – a refusal to give up. A refusal to let anger and violence win.

I don't always name my paintings – it feels pretentious – but I named this one Heddwch – the Welsh word for Peace. It felt appropriate somehow.

QUESTIONS:

1. How do your emotions, thoughts and feelings affect your creativity?
2. What music do you listen to? What films do your watch? What books do you read? How do these affect you? Emotionally? Creatively?
3. When are you at your most playful and imaginative?

4. What three words would describe the sort of life you would like to envision for yourself (e.g. creative, love, balance)? What can you do today to move towards making them a reality? Write them somewhere prominently, perhaps above your desk.

AFFIRMATION:
I channel my imagination and vision to live my best possible life.

CHAPTER NINE: THE SINGER, NOT THE SONG – THE CREATIVE EGO

Why do we create anything? It might be that you're driven by an innate desire to express yourself. Perhaps creativity is a sort of therapy, helping you to deal with and record difficult emotions. In that case, you may have no desire at all to share the results of your creativity with anyone – and that's absolutely fine.

On the other hand, you might decide you want to share your creativity with the world. In which case, if you're anything like me, you'll almost certainly find yourself torn between two conflicting fears. I call them The Terrible Two. Here they are:

The Terrible Two:

Fear Number One: What If I'm not good enough?
This is that innate fear that whatever we produce will never be good enough to meet with others' approval. You might ask yourself questions like 'What's the point in my doing this when there are other people doing the same thing much more effectively?' 'Who do I think I am, pretending to be a proper writer/artist?' and 'Why would anyone be interested in what I have to say anyhow?'

Fear Number Two: What if I'm too good?
This is a less obvious fear. It's possible you've felt it without ever even realising. Let me explain. If you're

like me, you perhaps went through your entire school life trying to keep your head down and become invisible. Schoolyards are brutal places. Anything outside of the norm becomes an instant excuse to be picked on. Therefore, if you're good at something, or even just have a passion for it (except for sport, sport's okay), it's best to stay quiet about it. This is reinforced by parents and teachers: Don't boast. Don't make a fuss. Nobody likes a show-off. While this is okay advice in itself, the tendency, especially for a natural people-pleaser like me, is to go too far in the opposite direction. We end up afraid to share anything at all, for fear of being seen as an egotistical show-off.

The reality is that you're probably somewhere between these two extremes. It's quite possible to suffer both extremes at once – simultaneously feeling like you're not good enough, and at the same time worrying about whether you'll set a false expectation if you do too well!

So...how can you ditch the Terrible Two?

'What If I'm Not Good Enough?' – Being Authentic

I once asked an extremely skilled musician, 'How did you get to be so good?' 'Oh, that's easy,' he replied. 'I just kept on playing the same wrong notes over and over until I didn't'.

This sums up the creative life. About 99 per cent of it is terrible first drafts, mistakes, red lines, false starts and restarts, crossings out, rubbing out and repainting. That leaves a magical one per cent that is pure inspiration! The challenge is to keep on polishing that jewel until it shines.

In a letter to her nephew James, written not long before her death, Jane Austen described her writing like this:

"What should I do with your strong, manly, spirited sketches, full of variety and glow? How could I possibly join them on to the little bit (two inches wide) of ivory on which I work with so fine a brush, as produces little effect after much labour?"

If even Jane Austen had to work on her first drafts, it is any surprise your first effort is not pure perfection? In the end, it's not about not being 'good enough'. It's a combination of soul – expressing what's innermost in your heart in the most authentic way possible – and practice. And if nobody likes it even then? Just remember that artists like Van Gough were never recognised in their own lifetime. And critics often get it wrong. For instance:

- **Walt Disney** was fired from the Kansas City Star in 1919 because, his editor said, he 'lacked imagination and had no good ideas'.
- After a performance at Nashville's Grand Ole Opry, **Elvis** was told by the concert hall

manager that he was better off returning to Memphis and driving trucks (his former career).
- During her lifetime, **Emily Dickinson** saw less than a dozen of her poems published out of about 1800 complete works.
- **Stephen King's** most renowned and first book, Carrie, was rejected thirty times. King decided to toss the book, which his wife then went through the trash to rescue and convinced him to re-submit it.
- While alive, **Monet's** work was mocked and rejected by the artistic elite, the Paris Salon.

Some artists have faced ridicule or outright contempt for being different. But what looks strange and different today might be just what's needed to break the mould. It's okay to break the rules and cross boundaries. Good art is not always commercial.

At the tender age of ten years old, Rayner Unwin used to act as a test reader for his father Stanley, who ran a publishing firm. Whenever a children's book came in, Stanley would give it to his son to read and, if he enjoyed it, it would be published. One of the books the young Rayner approved was Tolkein's The Hobbit, which was published in 1937.

Many years later, in 1951, Rayner, who was now a fully-paid employee, was handed the manuscript for The Lord of the Rings. He thought it ought to be published as well, and writing to his father with the figures, he said he thought they might lose a thousand pounds. Sir Stanley wrote back, saying 'If you think this to be a work of genius, then you may lose a thousand pounds.'[xxviii]

The work was published and, as they say, the rest is history.

So...if you have a creation vision, just do it. Don't worry about what others will think. Do it because it's burning a hole in your soul and you won't rest until it's out. Do it for any multitude of reasons, but don't do it for others' approval. Be your own whole, authentic self, like the child who dances even when nobody else it watching – because you need to. And practice, practice, practice, until you can create something you're happy with, something which sparkles with the light that is yours and only yours to give.

'What If I'm Too Good?' – Ego versus Self-Assurance

This one is perhaps better phrased 'But what if I become visible?' As I get older, I realise that I've spent a large proportion of my life trying to be invisible. As children, in particular, I think we're socially conditioned to fit in, to people-please, to not make a fuss. Sit down. Be quiet. Don't shout. Remember your please and thank-yous. Don't argue.

Stop complaining. Get your elbows off the table. Don't be bossy. Don't speak too loudly. Don't be difficult. At school and work we quickly learn that standing out in any way makes us a target. So we learn to button up and toe the line.

Unfortunately – or, perhaps, fortunately – I'm very bad at being invisible. As a teenager, the harder I tried to 'fit in' the more I stuck out. My clothes, my hair, my hobbies, my interests – nothing about me was remotely 'normal'. So eventually, I stopped trying. Bizarrely, it was when I finally stopped trying to fit in that I found people accepted me, or at least tolerated me. How had this happened?

It happened because I had learned to accept Myself.

Self-acceptance is very different to Ego. For a long time, I was very wary of any form of practice or meditation that spoke of 'abolishing the Ego'. After half a lifetime of trying to make myself invisible, I felt the last thing I needed was other people telling me to make myself smaller! But this was a misunderstanding on my part.

Ego and Self are not the same. The Ego is a false self we construct to try to cover for our own insecurities. It is the part of us we show to the world – our defensive 'mask', if you like. The Ego is desperate to be noticed by others, precisely because we have no secure sense of Self.

Once you learn to love yourself unconditionally, you will no longer depend on others for your sense of self-worth, security and validation. You will no longer feel like you have to compete with others to feel worthy.

Ego is an empty shell that masquerades as self-love.
Authentic Self-Love doesn't need others' approval.

Ego grabs the prize and shares it with no-one.
Self-love is self-assured enough to want to share the prize with others.

Ego is an emptiness that constantly needs filling.
Self-love is a permanent state of calm, self-assurance.

Ego boasts of achievements and dominates conversations.
Self-love is calmly confident and happy to learn by listening to others.

Ego wants everything for itself.
Self-love can afford to be generous.

So here's the thing. It's okay – in fact, it's more than okay, it's essential – to love yourself! Despite everything you may have been told about holding back and considering others and not being a bother, it's actually okay to admit that, deep down, you love doing what you do and, yes, you're good at it, and it's okay to want to share that talent with others.

If you are truly confident in your own abilities, you won't need to worry about pleasing others. Life will no longer feel like a competition or a constant battle. In fact, you can afford to be generous when it comes to sharing your talents with others.

Bizarrely, when you stop trying to please everybody else and 'fit in', that will probably be the time when they suddenly 'get' you. And even if they didn't, well at least you got to be authentic!

I just wish I'd learned it a whole lot earlier.

Going Deeper: Lessons on dealing with ego

Lesson One: You are the song, not the singer

I grew up in a folky family. Music, arts, drama and creativity were a natural part of my childhood. My parents weren't houseproud. We had lots of pets – a dog, a cat, goats, ducks – and both of us children were constantly making things out of sticky tape, cardboard tubes, pens and bits of paper. My Mum made patchwork quilts for our beds so the kitchen table was often covered with squares of fabric. Our house was a gorgeous, chaotic colourful confusion of muddy pawprints, over-excited children and half-completed artistic creations. Visitors came and went and brought with them their own forms of creativity – music, arts, drama and dance. A wooden stool in my parents' living room is still pock-marked with little dents from where it was used as a drum with spoons for beaters at a one of my parents' parties.

To help pay the bills, my parents took in lodgers, often foreign students– two French women, an Italian who cooked us delicious spaghetti Bolognese, Uncle Ali – my favourite – a wonderful, larger-than-life Yemeni man who spoke very little English but delighted in listening to our kids' fairytales, and who experienced his first ever snowstorm with the wide-eyed wonder of a child. All of these people shared their cultures and creativity with us, and us with them. So, for me, it was natural and normal that creativity was something to be shared together – a reciprocal act of giving and receiving. There was never any competitiveness, or a need to be 'better' than others, or to seek praise. In fact, the best praise anyone could ever give you was to join in.

Looking back, I can see how this has coloured my approach to creativity all through life. In the folk clubs I attended later as a student, it was unusual for anyone to come up afterwards and praise your singing or playing ability. Instead, it was much more normal for them to say 'I loved that song – what was it?' or 'Could you tell me the name of that tune and the source, so I can learn it?' Creativity was communal – a giving and sharing.

Even today, I'd still far rather someone tell me 'I loved that song' and 'That poem really moved me' than be told 'That was a great performance'. Because it isn't a performance. Not really.

'Performance' suggests a separation of the singer from the song. But the reality is that it is not about me. My job is not to make myself look good. It is to share the song, poem, or whatever other form of creativity I have to offer.

I am the Song, not the Singer.

Which leads me onto…

Lesson Two: Soli Deo Gloria – SDG

'I play the notes as they are written but it is God who makes the music.' – Johann Sebastien Bach.

The composer Bach showed promise from an early age. Born into a family of musicians, he quickly learned to sing and played several instruments. But his early success was hit by tragedy, with both his parents dying before he was ten. Johann got his first job as an organist aged just 17, but even then, there were conflicts with the church leaders. They complained that his pieces were too complicated for the choir to cope with. The young composer even ended up in a street fight with a choir member, who he'd branded a 'nanny goat bassoonist'! He moved to another church, and a new conflict. The Pietist parishioners in the church demanded more simple music – something that would draw attention to God and not to the music itself. A frustrated Bach protested that his aim was to create 'well-regulated church music to the glory of God'.

JS Bach went on to undertake a series of music-related jobs, married twice, fathered seven children, and by the time he died, aged 65, had completed over 1000 musical compositions. But he never forgot that early conflict. Every one of his surviving musical manuscripts has the letters SG – which stands for Soli Deo Gloria (To The Glory of God Alone) – written in the corner.

You don't need to have any religious faith to appreciate the value of Bach's story. When he was working under his own power – composing showy pieces to impress an audience – it just didn't seem to work for him. Something important was missing. It was only when he turned his attention away from himself and back to the source of the music that things began to fall into place.

It's the difference between performing a song and actually *singing* it. When I think I perform a poem,

I'm automatically putting up a barrier. I am the Performer, those listening are my Audience (and see how patronising that sounds?!). But when I *share* it – when I open myself up to the vulnerability of letting others into my space – that's when the magic happens. It's as if you pull up a chair and the Muse – breath, inspiration, creative energy, call it what you will – quietly walks in and sits alongside you.

When this happens, the audience ceases to be an audience. You cease to be a performer. For a moment, time itself stops and you become one with the energy of the universe, in a mutual understanding which crosses all cultural barriers. *Soli Deo Gloria.*

That, my friends, is when the magic happens.

That is when you become the Song.

QUESTIONS:

1. Which of these speaks to you more strongly: Fear of not being good enough or fear or being too good? Or a mix of the two?
2. How have childhood experiences influenced your sense of who you are? Do you feel under constant pressure to please others?
3. How do you relate to the idea of 'becoming the song'?

4. What techniques could you use today to improve your confidence in sharing your work?

AFFIRMATION:

I am the Song, not the singer.

CHAPTER TEN: FINDING FLOW

The Principle of Flow – How being untidy taught me a valuable lesson

I've been very busy this week, having a big clearout. One of the perils of living in a small house and being a parent is the sheer amount of clutter that accumulates very quickly! I must admit, I'm a bit of a magpie, with an eye for a bargain and a trawler of charity shops, which definitely doesn't help! I also have a tendency to hoard, which is something I'm working on.

I've read books on minimalism and come to the conclusion that it's only possible if you eat out, create nothing, have no partner and no kids! But while I'm probably never going to be a minimalist (my book collection alone sees to that!), I am slowly improving. One of the things I've found really helpful in getting rid of unnecessary stuff is a secret I'd like to share with you. I call it the Principle of Flow.

Simply put, everything around us is in a constant state of flux. We like to think of time as linear, but it isn't, it's cyclical. There's a reason why clocks have round faces, not square ones. It's human nature to want to hold onto things, but that's not the way the world is. Every day I'm getting older, my life is changing. Nothing ever stays still.

Our possessions are there to serve us. The purpose of books is to be read. The purpose of a lovely coat is to be worn. But if my books are sitting on the shelf no longer being read, they have lost their sense of purpose and become a dry, dead thing.

If my coat is hanging in my wardrobe never to be worn, it might just as well not exist. Once my things have lost their sense of purpose, it's time for them to move on, and serve somebody else. No matter how much I once loved them, I have cut off their flow.

I am writing this in September, a time when parents are waving goodbye to their children at school gates or watching their bigger children take their first steps into adulthood as they leave home and go to university. Such partings are painful. It's something, if I'm honest, I fear. Yet, even now, I'm already preparing my daughter for greater independence, teaching her the skills she will need to survive without me. I wouldn't be a good parent if I didn't. As creators, we're an essential part of the flow. Ideas come to us, sometimes with a whisper, sometimes with a shout, and we have to make them live – on paper, on screens, or on canvas. If we refuse to do so, perhaps through fear of not getting it right or worrying about how others might respond, we kill off the idea at source.

Once I've turned the idea into something concrete, I then have to set it free, to let it make its own way in the world, independently of myself. The execution of the idea was mine, and mine alone, but the spark that provoked it exists outside of me, and will go on beyond me. That's part of the cycle of life. As creative people, we get our sparks out there into the world, and if we've done our job, they spread and light a fire of their own.

It's part of us, too. We're born, we live, if we're lucky, eighty or ninety years or so, but ultimately we die. We don't get to take our possessions or our ideas with us. They were never really ours in the first place. But the sparks we leave behind – the words, the memories, the seeds we've sown and the love we've shown – those things live on, grow, and multiply in the lives of others.

Those things are eternal.

Taoism and Wu Wei – The art of non-action

'That which offers no resistance, overcomes the hardest substances. That which offers no resistance can enter where there is no space. Few in the world can comprehend the teaching without words, or understand the value of non-action."
– Lao Tzu, Tao Te Ching, Chapter 43.

Taoism[xxix] is an ancient Chinese belief system which is based on the writings of Lao-Tzu, a sixth century BCE religious philosopher. It teaches that people should lead a simple, honest life and not interfere with the course of natural events.

The word Tao means 'the Way', the pattern and substance of everything that exists. Four basic teachings of Taoism are: Simplicity and compassion, going with the flow, letting go, and harmony.

A central principle of Taoism is the critical importance of non-action, or what is called 'Wu Wei' in Chinese philosophy.

This is the idea that, in life, rather than fighting against every obstacle that comes up against us, we can allow things to take their natural course. This means accepting the things we can't change and being prepared to be patient. Sometimes, inaction may be the best approach, rather than jumping at opportunities before we're properly prepared.

Imagine water flowing over a hard rock. To the outward eye, the rock is far stronger than the water. The water is soft, pliable, non-resistant. Yet the continuous persistent movement of the water will eventually wear down the rock so that, over time, entire cliffs may crumble.

The Tao Te Ching describes it like this:

"Water is fluid, soft, and yielding. But water will wear away rock, which is rigid and cannot yield. As a rule, whatever is fluid, soft, and yielding will overcome whatever is rigid and hard. This is another paradox: what is soft is strong." — Lao Tzu

Wu Wei is sometimes translated as 'effortless action' or the 'action of non-action'.

The process of creativity encompasses both action and non-action. If you're struggling and striving and feel like you're getting nowhere – perhaps you're stuck in a seemingly endless writers' block or no matter how hard you try, nothing seems to go right – then it's time to STOP!

Remember the principle of Wu Wei. Remember the power of the water, flowing effortlessly over the stone. Tap into your inner source of creative energy and strength. Stop striving and just be. It's okay. You've got this. You already have everything you need within you.

A Swimming Lesson

As a child, I hated swimming. I was skinny as a rake and hated wearing a swimming costume in front of my classmates. I had no natural buoyancy. I hated being wet. I hated being cold. When it came to school swimming lessons, I flailed about like an ant drowning in a puddle. I fought and fought against the water, splashing and kicking furiously in my panic to stay afloat. Until a more enlightened instructor told me: 'Don't panic. Lie back and you will naturally float. Trust the water.' So I did and, to my amazement, as soon as I stopped fighting against the water, I found I could float. Once I'd learned how to trust the water and work with the natural flow, not fight against it, I learned to swim.

Non-action – Wu Wei – is so much more than just doing nothing. It is about trusting rather than striving, cultivating inner stillness and strength, rather than battling against the universe. When we are able to do this, we open ourselves up to the Tao – the creative energy that runs through everything (creative inspiration, which means 'in-breathed-ness'). Relax. Breathe it in. Just…breathe.

What does being in the flow feel like?

Athletes and runners call it being 'in the zone'. It's that moment when all the months and years of training finally pay off, when, instead of feeling like you're constantly striving, you find your body moving strongly, determinedly, where you feel entirely focused and free.

Perhaps you've experienced it as a writer, when you start creating something and the book, story or poem you are writing seems to start writing itself. Hours can pass with you barely noticing and, writing, for once, feels effortless and completely natural.

Or perhaps you've found yourself caught up in some other activity – sewing or dancing or music or gardening or knitting or craft, and found yourself totally absorbed in the moment, oblivious to everything around you. A musician friend described it to me as 'the moment when the instrument starts to play you.'

A word of caution:

It's impossible to live in a state of flow all the time. There will be times – many times – when you feel like a trainee runner, struggling against yourself, watching other more successful people race on past to the finish line, wondering why on earth you ever started this project, full of self-doubts and worries, struggling even to breathe. But just like an athlete or professional dancer, the more you train, the better you learn the steps, the easier and more natural it becomes.

Read and read and read until the rhythms of poetry become lodged in your head. Then read some more. Do writing exercises. Try out different forms; set yourself regular challenges, just for fun. Ninety per cent of what you write will be nonsense. Keep writing anyway. Like the upper layers of a pond, most of what's on the surface will be full of leaves and grime and all sorts of rubbish. But underneath, in the inner depths, you will find clear, pure water.

If you find yourself struggling too hard, then stop. Take a breather. Allow yourself time to just 'be'.

Listen to music that uplifts you. Take a bath or shower. Go for a walk in the park. Treat yourself to something nice – you deserve it. Be kind to yourself. Reconnect to the inner source of your power. Trust.

None of your exercises or practice are in vain. When the time is right for you to create again, all of those rhythms and the music and beauty you have absorbed will write themselves naturally onto the page. The ideas will flow – as easily and naturally and simply as water rushing over pebbles on the beach. It may not happen all the time. It may, in fact, only happen very rarely. But when it does, it's the most wonderful feeling in the world. This is what it feels like to be 'in the flow'. Magical, isn't it?

Real-life tips: How do others get 'in the flow'?

I asked some of my creative friends how they get 'in the flow' when writing or creating. Here are some of their responses:

- 'When lost in my imagination, vivid images flow, for example, the gush of a waterfall, rumbling thunder' – BM, Indian poet
- 'Wake up, drink a black coffee and pick up a pen and paper before I bathe or anything else. The awake but still slightly dreamy state is perfect.' – SB, poet and songwriter.

- 'I have a rack full of CDs that have no discernible rhythm and no lyrics; they dissolve time. I sit in my armchair at the window overlooking the park. I drink my tea and let the sounds wash over me. Within the hour, I've opened my mind to the creative current and I'm at my desk, typing away for the rest of the day – it just takes those first few minutes to let go of the day-to-day and let the mind find its way back to the path.' – BH, poet.
- 'Drink (sometimes), read poetry (preferably not like mine), listen to music (noise-cancelling headphones), or run ideas plus sound-patterns, speech-rhythms and syntactic/prosodic structures in my head.' – CN, poet.
- 'Wake up and not to think too much, and write first thing.' – GWD, poet.
- 'Mornings are best or walks in the forest, allow me to mentally process creativity, generating notes on the phone. I also use pictures to generate writing.' – MDCS, poet.
- 'I like to listen to other artists for inspiration. Though for me, I can never force it, it just comes to me and when it does, it flows itself.' – MS, songwriter.
- 'I like writing at the library. Or anywhere not associated with day-to-day life.' – AS, poet.

WORKSHOP: MEDITATION WRITING EXERCISE

Taking the idea of the river as a metaphor, try this meditation:

It is a calm summers day. The sun is shining, and you are sitting on a river bank, looking out across a beautiful sparkling river. You can hear birdsong. A gentle breeze is blowing. As you look out across the water, you notice how the light dances upon the surface, and when you look deeper you can see that the water beneath is pure and perfectly clear. You feel a strong sense of wellbeing and peace. You start to feel drowsy and as you settle your head back onto the soft grassy riverbank, you realise that the river represents your creative life. Looking back, you can see how far you've come, and looking forward you can see where you are headed. This part of the river represents your current reality.

Where are you on the river? Where are you creatively? Personally? Is the water clear and smooth or exciting and fast-moving? Are you facing unexpected bends or obstacles? Are there treacherous rocks or crocodiles lurking beneath the surface? Is the water shallow or deep? Are you alone or are there others with you on your journey? Are you heading out towards the open sea, or are you still at the beginning of your adventure? Is the water clear and pure or muddy and full of debris? Can you see an end in sight? Where is your destination?

When you feel ready, open your eyes. Think about the river. Think about how far you've travelled, and all the adventures you still have to enjoy. Thank the river for everything it has brought you so far, for the obstacles you've faced and overcome, and for the companions who have guided you on your journey. Thank the river for everything it will bring you in the future. Trust the river to keep you in the flow of your deepest, most authentic creative self.

Afterwards, perhaps write down some of your observations, or draw them, or make a poem out of them. If you're feeling really creative, you could even draw some of them out as a shape poem based on different parts of a river, for example whirlpools, ripples or meanders.

QUESTIONS:

1. Can you remember a time when you felt fully 'in the flow'? How did it feel?
2. What sorts of activities or environments can help you get in the flow?
3. What could you practically do to get yourself into this flow state more often?
4. How well do you relate to the Chinese idea of 'wu wei' – the concept of 'active non-action'? Do you find it helpful or a hinderance?

AFFIRMATION:

I step into the flow of creativity. I let the words run freely.

CHAPTER ELEVEN: SENSES AND SENSIBILITY

An Ordinary Mind on an Ordinary Day...

The year is 1919. Aged 37, just after the success of her first novel, 'Voyage Out' and while awaiting publication of her second novel 'Night and Day', Virginia Woolf is invited to write an essay 'Modern Fiction' for the Times Literary Supplement.[xxx]

'Examine for a moment an ordinary mind on an ordinary day', she writes. 'The mind receives a myriad impressions – trivial, fantastic, evanescent, or engraved with the sharpness of steel.'

She invites us to use all our senses – to write not just a single narrative but a series of inter-connecting narratives, the inner and outer dialogues of the writer. Virginia Woolf is not just interested in what we can see, hear and touch but what the author thinks as well – and what those she observes are thinking, too.

The result is a multi-layered prose, which, at first feels overwhelming, even confusing. When you first read Virginia Woolf's novels, it's a bit like reading a poem. Ideas are expressed in ways that are not always linear or logical. It is writing as the author perceives the world – painting pictures with words. Multi-layering image upon image, so that we don't just see the world as she perceives it, we start to feel it, too. She describes it like this:

'Life itself is not a series of gig lamps symmetrically arranged; life is a luminous halo, a semi-transparent envelope surrounding us from the beginning of consciousness to the end'.

Stop. Look. Listen. What can you see? Hear? Taste? Feel?

Stop.

Look

Approximately 80 per cent of everything we learn comes through our eyes.

The eye contains over two million working parts and is one of the most complex organs in the body, second only to the brain.

Stop.

Look. Really look. What do you see?

Take a moment to appreciate what is happening beyond your immediate frame of vision – the wide open space, sky and trees. Notice colours, textures, movements and stillness.

Now focus on what is right in front of you – your close vision. Really focus in. Notice the tiny details –

cracks in the wood, pockmarks and surface dents. Notice textures. Notice how the light moves across the surface, or how tiny flickers of breeze catch the curtains and create a rippling effect. Go in really close. Look at a particular object – a coffee cup or glass or water. Observe it like an artist. Where does the light fall? What shapes or reflections do you see? Is it hard or soft? Write down some descriptive phrases.

Now go wider. Notice your peripheral vision – everything that happens at the sides of your vision. How aware are you of your surroundings? How many small details are missed each day?

Blur your eyes slightly and notice how your vision changes. Then open them wide and appreciate the sharpness of perfect vision. Be grateful for the blessing of sight.

Listen

Close your eyes and listen to the sounds around you. Perhaps you are somewhere peaceful but you hear birds in the trees. Perhaps there are the sounds of children playing, sirens wailing, or the dim rumble of traffic. Perhaps you are somewhere busy like a café with clinking cups, conversation and background music. Notice how many sounds you filter through your world every day. If are able to get somewhere really peaceful, listen out for micro sounds – the inhale and exhale of your own breath. Hum quietly, or sing a single note. Notice how the sound vibrates physically. Consider how the sound of your own voice connects with the vibrations of the universe. Consider what sounds bring harmony and which are discordant. How can you bring greater harmony into your world? Sit down quietly and write down every sound you hear.

Smell

Smell can be a neglected sense, but it is one of the most evocative. Smells are said to evoke memories better than any other sense. What smells do you associate with your childhood, or with a special event such as a wedding or family occasion? Take time to appreciate the scents immediately around you. Perhaps you smell cut grass or earth or ground coffee, or last night's dinner? Think about what scents you find pleasant or unpleasant. What smells are precious to you? Are there odd smells which you love (one of my favourites is the smell of old books!)? Write a list of your favourite smells, or a poem which takes a particular smell as its starting point.

Taste

Did you know that the average adult has anywhere from 2,000 to 10,000 taste buds (our sense of taste diminishes as we get older, which is why little children are such fussy eaters!) So often we eat and drink without really thinking about it or appreciating the tastes or flavours of what we consume. So take a moment to eat or drink something mindfully. Perhaps take inspiration from Chinese tea-making ceremonies and make yourself the perfectly blended cup of tea, drunk of course from your best china. Or eat a slice of apple or piece of fruit. What do you taste? Is it tangy, sour or sweet? How does texture affect your enjoyment? Is it soft? Crunchy? Think about your favourite tastes – and your worst. Set aside time throughout the day to fully appreciate what you're eating or drinking.

Touch

Touch is the most delicate of all the senses. Thousands of nerve endings in the skin respond to four basic sensations – pressure, hot, cold and pain. When we are born, the first sensation we experience is that of physical touch. A warm hug from a person we love feels safe and secure. But sometimes touch can feel uncomfortable. Perhaps there are certain textures or fabrics that make our skin crawl, or unwelcome touch which makes us feel unsafe. Think for a moment about the sensation of touch – how things feel, and how they make you feel. What textures do you find comforting or unlifting? Which are scratchy and uncomfortable? Perhaps create a 'touch box' of objects, close your eyes and register how each item feels – whether soft or hard, bumpy or smooth, warm or cold. Register the temperature of the air around you. Is it warm or cold, or is there a slight breeze? What is the most comfortable place you have ever known? (For me it was sleeping in a tiny tight booth in a canal boat, snuggled up tight with the sound of water lapping around my ears!) Take time to be thankful for the sensation of touch.

There are two other senses, in addition to the four you may be familiar with. These are:

Kinesthetic
Kinesthetic sense is about the connection between your sense and the world around you. Typically, it involves movement. For example, spinning on a merry-go-round, or the sense of the wind rushing past you when riding on a horse.

Organic
Organic sense is awareness of your inner bodily functions. For example, breathing, pulse, heartbeat, or muscle tension.

- *How do you feel when you think about the various different senses?*
- *Does one sense connect particularly strongly with you?*

- *Experiment with writing using different senses. Perhaps write about a favourite sight, sound or smell which evokes strong memories of an event or person.*

Dylan Thomas's Holiday Memory – A Fanfare of Sunshades Opening

Dylan Thomas's Holiday Memory, first published in 1972, is one of my favourite pieces of writing, and another great example of writing using all of the senses. A nostalgic look back at a day by the seaside on a sunny August Bank Holiday, the words invoke vivid imagery, so much so that you can almost taste the grit of sand in the sandwiches.

Though not a poem, it plays with words and images in a way that is very like poetry. For example:

'Recalcitrant uncles huddled, over lukewarm ale, in the tiger-striped marquees. Mothers in black, like wobbling mountains, gasped under the discarded dresses of daughters who shrilly braved the gobbling waves'.

There's some clever mixing of familiar phrases with new ones, to create something surprising, especially at the start:

'August Bank Holiday – a tune on an ice-cream cornet. A slap of sea and a tickle of sand. A fanfare of

sunshades opening. A wince and whinny of bathers dancing into deceptive waters…A silent hullabaloo of balloons'.

Reread the piece and notice how many senses the writer evokes – from scratchy towels to gritty sandwiches, the sound of dialogue (some of which is quoted verbatim), the softness of the sand and the sponge cake, the 'smell of the vinegar on shelled cockles' and 'the noise of the pummeling Punch and Judy falling'.

Now think of a familiar or memorable event – perhaps a wedding, a birthday party, or a family outing. List all the sights, scents, smells, tastes and sounds you associate with this event. Think, too, about how you moved, how your body responded, how you felt.

Respond in whatever way you like – writing, painting, drawing or music – using and evoking as many senses as you can.

You can find a copy of Dylan Thomas's Holiday Memories online at: www.drownedinsound.com

WRITING WORKSHOP: SENSE WRITING

Sense writing – otherwise known as object writing – is a timed writing exercise, in which you focus on describing an object or event, using all your senses.

The technique was first described by Berklee College of Music professor and songwriting expert Pat Pattinson in his 1995 book, *Writing Better Lyrics.*

The exercise is simple. Take an object or event – for example, a cup, a window, or a flower (I used a funfare ride for mine. See Prompts at the end of the chapter).

Focus on this object with all your senses – sight, hearing, smell, sound, taste, touch, plus kinesthetic (movement) and organic (heartbeat, breathing and muscle tension). Don't hold back on any thoughts or feelings and don't worry, for the moment, about how the words flow together, grammar or spelling. The aim is to write down the first thoughts and images that come into your mind, focusing on all your senses. (You could focus on each sense individually, or just let them run into one another).

Do this exercise for exactly 10 minutes and then reread what you've written. Perhaps there are certain words or phrases that stand out, which you could develop as part of a longer piece, either as a poem, a piece of prose, or a song. If you are an artist, perhaps something you've written evokes a particular image which you could use to create a visual representation of your feelings?

Feel the Music
It's worth noting that Object Writing started life as a way of writing lyrics. Think about how the way you

perceive the world through your senses affects the way you understand the world, and other people. A song is a poem in music. When you listen to a song, or a poem, or look at a painting, or watch a play or a dance, you are participating in a shared experience. You are glimpsing the world – in some small part – as someone else has seen it. For one small moment, time and geography cease to matter, as you are part of something bigger, something universal. That's the magic of creativity.

What music will you add to the world?

Object Writing Example (unedited)

Funfair Ride

The smell of tramped earth, creosote, diesel, candyfloss. Lights whir in dizzying motion, an overwhelm of the senses. A plastic polar bear caught in a ring of disco fire, framed by artificial ice crystals. Alongside the ride, another plastic bear receives hugs and pouts for Instagram selfies, his face contorted in frozen rage. Recalling the taste of winters past. Candyfloss which clung to hair and dissolved invitingly on the tongue. Overpriced candies, roast chestnuts and Belgian waffles thick with artificial cream. The taste of fear, excitement, anticipation, at being spun, dazzled, whirled into oblivion that may or may not ever end. A questioning of reality, a letting go of inhibitions, a willingness to be bedazzled. The music swells as the carts begin, slowly at first, to rock and then spin. Crescendo of screams as each cart is sent spinning horizontally, defiance of gravity, fear mingled with whoops of joy until it's hard to tell which is which. 'We Will Rock You' chants the soundtrack, a maniacal pre-recorded laugh, a clown's cackle, leering, cajoling, mocking. A shriek as the thing lurches to a halt, then starts up again – this time, backwards. Somebody screams 'let me out!' but there's no way out, souls and spirits sent spinning heavenwards. Heartbeats quicken, muscles tense, until heartbeat and music pulse become indistinguishable. A thudding in the ears, in the throat, in the temple. Hands grip sweaty metal constraints, fingers tremble. A vibration that thuds through your entire body until you can take no more, and then...it slows, it screeches to a halt. You are left wondering what just happened, if any of it made sense, if any of it was real, but a thought suddenly strikes you: 'I am Alive!' You descend, grinning from the ride, the words already rising to your lips: 'Again! Again!'

Object Writing Prompts:
Objects – cup, water, vase, table, curtains, window, a thing you treasure, handbag, doors, an item of clothing, moon, sun, clouds, flower, butterfly, cat, dog, blanket.
People – daughter, mother, father, son, teacher, the most eccentric person you ever met, my hero, politician, an inspiring historical figure, farmer, dancer, nun, boxer, magician, cleaner, actor, king, first love, homeless person, singer, judge.

Places – your first home, workplace, holiday destination, town, countryside, museum, park, prison, religious building, derelict building, kitchen, graveyard, classroom, hotel, heaven, hell, outer space, frontline.

Times/Events – wedding, funeral, first day at school, becoming a parent, falling in love, moving out, first day, sunrise, sunset, lunch bell, saying sorry, wildfire, earthquake, war.

Emotions – happy, sad, angry, disappointed, scared, love, infatuation, nostalgia, boredom, humility, horror, terror, nervous, impatient, uncertain.

Concepts – ageing, beauty, death, birth, affair, cold, tradition, shadow, dream, forgiveness, news, hope, peace.

QUESTIONS:

1. When you write, which sense is normally most prominent? Have a go experimenting with writing from different senses, and differing perspectives.
2. How aware are you of your senses? This week, practice being more aware of every sense, movement and sensations.

AFFIRMATION: **I use all of my senses to create.**

CHAPTER TWELVE: MASKS AND MIRRORS – IDENTITY AND SELF IMAGE

'Tell us a little about yourself'

The old, familiar feeling of dread rises, a curled knot in the stomach as, one by one, your colleagues or co-workers reel off exciting achievements and witty anecdotes. Suddenly, it's your turn. The room goes silent with anticipation. You reel and twist in your seat. Your mouth goes dry. You begin:

'Well...there's not much to say, really...'

It's odd, isn't it? There's a strange kind of irony that, as someone who has worked in marketing, I can sell anything to anybody, but I can't sell my own achievements or talents. Interviews are a particular form of sub-terranean nightmare, specifically designed to intimidate socially awkward introverts like me. I don't tick any of the normal boxes or fit any of the questions neatly. I've spent three-quarters of my working life self-employed (this is probably why!) I'm not a team player; I work best on my own, and I'm bad at taking instruction. And on top of it all, I'm too honest. When asked 'Where would you like to be in ten years' time?' 'Living in an artistic commune with a herd of goats' never seems to be the answer they were looking for.

From a very early age, especially as women, we're taught not to shout too loud, not to boast of our achievements or push ourselves forward. When teams were being selected at school, I was always the last to be chosen, the awkward, shy, skinny kid who nobody wanted, the captains of both teams arguing: 'No, you can have her.'

Perhaps I'm overthinking here. It's a fault of mine. I vividly remember, several years ago, meeting a male poet, a hero of mine, whose work I much admired, at a workshop. At the end of the writing session, when we had each read out and discussed our pieces of work, he turned to me rather haughtily and told me: 'You think too much'. Perhaps I do. Perhaps all women do. I blame it on Eve. If you look back at the story in Genesis, it wasn't the Tree of Life she stole from but the Tree of Knowledge. Eve's sin was a thirst for knowledge. That's not such a bad thing, surely? Perhaps those in positions of power have always secretly feared knowledgeable women.

Am I overthinking?

The best compliment anyone has ever given me was after I read poetry at an open-air market. One of the stall-holders came up to me and said: 'I like you. You have an interesting mind'. An interesting mind. I aspire to have an interesting mind.

Who am I? Why do I struggle so hard to share this?

Perhaps it's because I am so many people. Like everyone, I wear many different roles, often at the same time. I am Mother, wife, peace activist, writer, editor, Quaker, joker and jester, counsellor, singer, artist, musician, cook, cleaner, journalist, artist...and many, many more. I am all of these things but none of them completely and often feel like an imposter in my own life. Often, I feel as if I am spinning a thousand china plates in the air all at once and at any moment one or all of them might drop and I will be revealed as the failure I really am. (I am Resilient, I am Strong. I am an Adult, even though I often don't feel like one. I am almost certainly some form of neurodivergent. I am Dreamer. I am Idealist. I am Poet).

Masks

In order to deal with the strangeness of the world, I wear many masks. Often, I feel like a stranger in an alien world, born in the wrong place or the wrong century. The world is too fast, it is too fierce and aggressive for people like me. It is full of angry headlines, busy-ness, noise of distant wars and closer arguments. Online voices jostle for attention in an angry bustle of noise that never seems to switch off. I was not born for this angry world. Which of us ever was? And yet I realise that there are many people around the world for whom a life as secure and safe as mine is a luxury. We don't get to choose the world we're born into or the situations we face. So we put on masks. We perform the roles we have to perform, and we survive. If we're lucky, we get to keep the plates in the air. Sometimes, others applaud. But inside, we know we're really all just pretending.

Behind the Mask

Carnival players, we try our many masks on for size,
You are Harlequin, revelling in slapstick,
I your Columbine, unattainable and proud;
Now, you are Pierrot and I Pierette,
Nursing heartache in our golden-painted tears,
Our faces white and immoveable.

You ask if I am okay,
'Fine,' I say, and with every syllable,
Feel the mask closing in a little tighter.
'Look at me! Laugh at me!' you say,
Turning a heel on a banana skin,

Even whilst the tears
Spill through the cracks
In the mask.

Mirrors

Who do I see when I look in the mirror? Appearance plays such a huge role in this life. I know this, because every day I'm bombarded with adverts telling me how I should look – so it must matter. But a part of me really wishes it didn't. A part of me really wishes, just for once, I could not care. I envy those who don't care – crazy-haired eccentrics, and hippies at festivals in pyjamas and wellies, and dogs with loopy fur and misshapen ears. I am drawn to broken things. I rescue things from charity shops – odd paintings that nobody wants, weird shirts that are so ugly I want to wear them and make them feel loved again. I think of the little Me in the line waiting to be selected for the netball team. I think I am beginning to understand.

What do I see when I look in the mirror? I see a woman who is not perfect. I see lines, I see wrinkles, I see scars from mental and physical battles. I see all the mistakes I have made. I see the crease on my forehead and around my eyes – the frowns, the worry lines, from all that fearing and trying to please, to be enough but not too much, from trying to be clever but not too clever, from trying to fit into a world that doesn't fit me – from all that loving, all that needing, all that *thinking*.

'You think too much'...

Perhaps I do. One day soon, I hope, I shall look in the mirror and see a confident, self-assured woman who is not afraid to acknowledge past mistakes – someone who has learned through time and struggle. I shall see past the imperfections to the smiles and laughter lines. I shall see someone who is unafraid to say, determinedly: 'This is Me – who I love. This is who I have become'.

Bob Marley was once asked if there was a perfect woman. He replied: ' Who cares about perfection? Even the moon is not perfect. The sea is incredibly beautiful but salty and dark. The sky is infinite, but often cloudy. Everything that is beautiful isn't perfect; it's special. Every woman can be perfect to someone.'

Voice

What is your voice when you write? What is your voice when you sing?

I once lost my voice for six months. For half a year, I could utter nothing above a whisper. You never really appreciate your voice, until it's gone.

I've always been softly spoken. I envied those with louder, deeper voices, who could dominate a conversation. In open forums or at social gatherings, I was always afraid to speak in case nobody could hear me. (Next time you attend an open forum discussion, take note of how many women speak and how many men. How many others are equally intimidated?) Performing poetry and singing taught me that I, too, have a right to be listened to. Now, I try to encourage others to have their voices heard. I see it as part of my mission – to encourage new voices, to provide a platform, to say 'You, yes you! Your voice matters!'

What is your voice?
Is it soft or loud, gentle or strong? The folk singer Karen Dalton once said 'In order to be heard, you have to learn to sing softer'. Once I heard an entire busy pub silenced by a single, pure note.

Your voice is more powerful than you know.

How will you use it?

How will you use your beautiful, powerfully gentle voice?

Know Thyself – An inner and outer journey

Writing is a dangerous activity. It risks exposing our weaknesses. The writer F Scott Fitzgerald once said 'What people are ashamed of usually makes a good story'. We are all full of stories – both good and bad. Stories that can shed light on the human condition and help others going through similar experiences. Stories that can inspire. Stories that can entertain.

Writing makes us vulnerable. It risks giving away too much. It's like that irritating colleague at the Christmas party who insists on over-sharing. Sometimes, I wish I'd stop. Creating invites critique. It invites criticism. A poetry open mic is the only place I can think of (apart from possibly an AA meeting) where you walk into a room full of strangers, pour out the innermost workings of your soul, and sit down again.

Writers are dangerous people. There's a reason fascist regimes burn books. Writers open up boxes of thoughts that ought not to be opened. They make us feel. They make us remember that we are really just souls in pretty packages. They cause us to question all the truths we've been told to hold dear – that earning money and gathering possessions can make us happy, that those in positions of power have all the answers, that we ought to compete over limited resources rather than sharing what we've been blessed with, that some people hoarding wealth while others have barely enough to survive is the natural way of things. Writers make us question these so-called truths, envisage new truths and ask *'What if?'*

Artists and musicians are dangerous, too. I heard the composer Karl Jenkins interviewed on the radio last night. The interviewer criticised him for composing music for adverts: 'Isn't that emotional manipulation?' she asked. The composer replied: 'Isn't that what all music does?' Music, Art and Writing are dangerous. They evoke emotions. Emotions are dangerous – uncontrollable.

Creativity exposes the soul. It leaves us bare. But it also communicates to others. It invites everyone to feel more deeply. It creates connection. It creates community.

WORKSHOP: WRITING EXERCISES

If I were a poem
How would you describe yourself to someone who had never met you? Think not just in physical terms but in terms of your personality, and the 'inner' you –

your likes and dislikes, quirks, interests, even your annoying habits! Write (or draw) the results.

A postcard to My future/past self
What would you say to the younger version of yourself? What advice would you give? What would you say to a future version of yourself? If you are feeling adventurous, write a letter to your future self. Put it in an envelope and open it in five years' time.

QUESTIONS

1. Who am I?
2. What sort of person am I?
3. What are my essential values and beliefs?
4. What are my visions? What are my dreams?
5. What stories have defined me?
6. Whose stories have I contributed to?
7. Who will I become?
8. What is my writing voice?
9. What is my speaking/ singing voice?
10. What prevents me from speaking my truth?

AFFIRMATION:

I reclaim my own, authentic self. I have a right to tell my story and be heard.

CHAPTER THIRTEEN: BEAUTY CAN CHANGE THE WORLD – WHY I WRITE

'Resistance and change often begin in art, and very often in our art, the art of words.'
— Ursula K Le Guinn

'Beauty can change the world' — Dostoyevsky

I was on my way to work. It had been a frustrating morning of missed connections and delays. It was pouring with rain and my shoes were soaking. The last thing I felt like was sitting through another dull meeting. And then I saw it. Pushing up between the concrete. Wedged in an impossibly thin line of earth, a tiny, bright yellow flower, its golden petals shining defiantly against the grey.

It felt like some kind of sign.

Beauty has a way of turning up, even in the most unexpected places. During lockdown, when I found myself at my bleakest, deprived of human company with a nightly new litany of deaths, I felt more frightened and isolated than I had ever been, and fell into a kind of depression. It was during those dark days that I found myself rediscovering the music of the Spirituals and the Blues. Those ancient voices, rising through the darkness of centuries of oppression and struggle suddenly spoke to me and started to make sense:

WRITE MINDFULLY

By the rivers of Babylon,
We sat down and wept;
How can we sing the Lord's song
In a strange land?'

How can we sing, when everything around us feels dark and strange and frightening?

And yet we did. In those strange, dystopian times, amid the gloomy headlines there was news footage of people in Italy coming out of their locked down homes onto their doorsteps, singing arias together.

I lived at the time in a small, Welsh terraced house. Though surrounded by houses on all sides, I'd never really spoken to any of my neighbours. One morning during lockdown I was hanging out my washing when I heard a pure, joyful chorus drifting over the breeze. It was one I knew from long ago, when I used to go to church:

'Lord, I lift your name on high!
Lord I love to sing your praises!'

I looked across the wall, to the backyard of the adjoining houses, and there was my neighbour. Singing from the bottom of his soul, a wide smile on his face. As I stood, I joined the chorus, in harmony:

'Words can't express, not even in part,
Of the depth of love that is owed
By this thankful heart'

For a few, beautiful moments, there we were – two strangers brought together by song, singing joyful harmonies in spite of the fear and sickness that had separated us from families, loved ones and friends. Beauty has a habit of turning up in the most unexpected places.

There have been many times in my life like this, times when I've been tempted to give up, overwhelmed by the sheer weight of feeling like I am constantly battling a world which feels alien and ugly. At such times, creativity, in all its forms, has been my saviour. Writing, music, dance, song, art – these are the things that bring us together, that make us Real.

I'm sometimes asked why I write. The simple answer is that I have to, I can't help it. There are so many thoughts and dreams and ideas and images running round my mind that I have to put them down somewhere, otherwise my head might explode!

There are so many things to be angry or frustrated or worried about: war and climate change and politicians who no longer seem to have our best interests at heart (if they ever did) and yet…and yet, in spite of it all, I choose to hope. I see signs of hope whenever those who care make their voices heard. I see inspirational, strong people with powerful messages and powerful lives. I often feel powerless to make a difference, but I can tell their stories and, hopefully, perhaps create something of beauty.

Can beauty change the world?

Perhaps it is the only thing that ever has.

Creative restlessness – finding time to just Be

Deep in my soul, I have a sort of creative restlessness – an endless drive to be constantly creating, always moving on to the next project and the next. It doesn't really matter to me what form the creativity takes. Sometimes it can be poetry, or editing, or composing a piece of music, or drawing. So long as I am creating, I'm fulfilled. Even when I try to sleep, my mind is often full of dozens of ideas – current projects and future ones – so that I find it almost impossible to switch off completely. Don't get me wrong: I love the fact my brain is buzzing with creative ideas. But there's a danger, too, that all this creative activity becomes too frenetic, too overwhelming, especially when coupled with perfectionism.

As creatives, we can often feel under pressure to be constantly producing, especially when we compare ourselves to other successful people. In today's 24/7 world, there's almost a bravado about working long and late. I remember people in the office I used to work in boasting about their 13-hour working days, in the same way as a student might boast of pulling an essay all-nighter. As we get older and face increasing demands at home and work, it's easy for creative activities to get squeezed out of our busy schedule.

We may even feel guilty for taking time out – as if every single second of our lives should be busy and productive. So, today I give you permission to STOP!

An important part of any creative process is taking time to step back, absorb, and allow ideas to incubate. It's also essential to our mental health. Human beings were never meant to spend 24 hours a day being constantly productive. We're animals, after all, and most animals spend much of their time resting. (If you don't believe me, take a look at your dog or cat!) Now I'm not suggesting you go full-on sloth (though if you need to, be my guest!), but grant yourself some time out, just to Be. Go to a local park. Watch the trees and the grass. You'd be amazed how teeming with life a single patch of grass can be! Feel the sunshine on your skin. Dance in the rain. Hear the rain as it splashes on the earth. Notice the colours and reflections of water. Go to a local café and just observe people. Hear their chatter like you'd hear birdsong, the rise and fall of speech, the inflections and the music it makes. Observe the interplay of emotions. Think of yourself as an Explorer of life. Allow yourself to be curious. Allow yourself to be childlike. Allow yourself to just Be.

These times of living are just as important as the heady bursts of creativity – probably more so. They allow us to sit and quietly absorb our surroundings before returning to the world reinvigorated. It is in these healing spaces that we enable our ideas to grow.

Resonance – Back to the Garden

'There is geometry in everything; there is music in the spacing of the strings' – Pythagorus.

Whose songs sing through you? The universe is a place of harmony. Everything, from the patterns of the seasons, to the rising and setting of the sun, to the rise and fall of the waves in line with the patterns of the moon, is carefully choreographed like a beautiful divine dance, perfectly syncopated to the rhythms of the universe. In the past, philosophers and mathematicians spoke of the music of the spheres (musica universalis). The theory, originating with Pythagorus in Ancient Greece, was later developed by 16th century astronomer Johannes Kepler in his Harmonices Mundi. Kepler believed that this harmony, while inaudible, could be heard by the soul and that it gave him a 'very agreeable feeling of bliss, afforded him by the music in the imitation of God'.

Such ideas might (or might not) seem fanciful to us today but, in fact, everything in the universe comes down to fine balance and harmony. When I walk in nature, I instantly feel a greater sense of music in my soul. I can feel it in the melodious sound of birdsong, the curving petals of a flower, in the way the sunlight catches at the ripples on a lake, the curling of a root or the shouting colours of a sunset. I don't need mathematical equations to tell me that the universe is a place of harmony. I know it, deep in my soul.

In physics, resonance is described as vibration that occurs at a frequency that causes other things to vibrate in synchronicity. If I pluck a string on a harp, the other strings around it vibrate in sympathy. This creates 'overtones' – beautiful harmonies we can only just hear, but we know they're there.
The whole universe is resonant. When I tap into the rhythms and harmony of nature, I feel instantly refreshed. As human beings, we are made to live in synch with the universe, rising when the sun rises and sleeping when it gets dark, eating what the earth produces and celebrating the changing seasons with time-held ritual and honour. It has never been more important to get back to the garden. Perhaps the very future of our planet depends upon it. We forget our place in the universe at our peril.

We need to get ourselves back to the garden – because that is where it all began. A voice, a resonance, hovered over the waiting waters, a voice that loved itself enough to want to be spoken and shouted and sung. That voice invites us now to pick up our pens and spin new stories into the world, stories that only we can tell, stories that can excite and ignite and inspire. Will you answer?

MANIFESTO

Art is a form of rebellion. At a time when there is much to grieve, much to make us feel dull or sad or drained, Art injects colour back into the world.
In the beginning was the **Word**.

Words are pure **magic**. Words are spelling. Words have power to create or destroy.
Arts says: We are here. Our voices matter.
Art gives voice to the voiceless and dispossessed. This is why fascists throughout history have burned books and paintings.
Art unites. **Music** is pure vibrational **energy**, emotion distilled into sound.
Art is the dance through which we live our shared experiences.

FIND YOUR VOICE
Share it powerfully.

Never let anybody tell you that you are not good enough.
You are more than enough. You are beautiful, precious, unique.
Nobody can tell your story better than you.

**So tell it, Sing it, Draw it,
Shout it, Dance it,
Live it! Be it!**

APPENDIX 1: THE AFFIRMATIONS

1. I embrace the blank page with excitement.
2. I grant myself permission to take time out. To simply Be.
3. I am part of a powerful cycle of creativity and inspiration.
4. I will keep on working until inspiration finds me.
5. Writing and creativity is as natural to me as breathing.
6. I am Enough. I am beautiful, powerful and unique. Nobody can tell my story as well as me.
7. I reclaim my right to be playful. I can be creative for the sheer joy of creating.
8. I channel my imagination and vision to live my best possible life.
9. I am the Song, not the singer.
10. I step into the flow of creativity. I let the words run freely.
11. I use all of my senses to create.
12. I reclaim my own, authentic self. I have a right to tell my story and be heard.
13. Beauty can save the world.

APPENDIX 2: WOMBWELL RAINBOW INTERVIEW

1. **What inspired you to write poetry?**
   I love words – the sound of them, the shape of them, the way they feel on my tongue, whether spoken or sung. I love the ability of words to jump off the page into my head and hold me spellbound when I listen, to capture a moment or movement in time. It's no coincidence that the word for 'enchantment' also means to sing – or that 'spelling' means to cast spells or put letters together to form words. Words are magic!

2. **Who introduced you to poetry?**
   My parents, by reading to me and encouraging me to read. When I was very young I used to love Dr Seuss and Edward Lear's nonsense verse. At primary school, I had a wonderful teacher called Mrs Baker who would march us all up and down the classroom reciting Captain Beaky and His Band. She understood me and would let me stop whatever I was doing to write. She used to slip me extra notebooks from the store cupboard to take home. When I was about seven, my parents took me and my brother to a poetry workshop run by Roger McGough. I remember him as this big hairy man who leapt around all over the place, reciting poems. He looked like he was enjoying himself

so much, I said to myself 'When I grow up, that's what I want to do'. When I had my first poetry collection published (Blood and Water, The Seventh Quarry, 2020) I tracked down my teacher Mrs Baker and sent her a copy with a card saying 'Thank you for believing in the dreams of a seven-year-old.' It took me over forty years but I finally did it – I achieved my ambition of becoming a published poet.

3. **How aware were you of the dominating presence of older poets?**
I wouldn't say this is a huge issue for me because I read a lot of work by up-and-coming young poets – people such as Natalie Ann Holborow, Sophie McKeand and Rufus Mufasa, whose work is fresh and exciting. That's not to say I don't like the more established poets too, though – we can learn so much from them. I joint-run Talisman Spoken Word open mic in Swansea with David Churchill (whose book Volcano Moon, I helped edit earlier this year). We have attenders from all ages, backgrounds and cultures. Our youngest is 16 and our oldest just turned 90! I feel lucky to be living in a vibrant city. Having such a wide mix of experiences enriches us all.

4. **What is your daily writing routine?**
I'm constantly juggling! My creative writing is sandwiched into tiny pockets of time, in

between proofreading and editing, a two-day-a-week day job, plus ferrying my daughter to and from school. Creative inspiration seems to come in sudden, short waves of energy, which often means doing some of my writing at odd hours such as the middle of the night. I don't necessarily recommend it!

5. **What motivates you to write?**
A lot of the earlier poems in my new collection, Blood and Water, have been inspired by my experiences of becoming a mother for the first time. It was a life-changing experience, profound! I'm inspired by all sorts of things – a word or phrase, a moment or feeling, nature, mythology... Writing gives me a voice and a way of processing things. Social issues drive me, too. A thirst for social justice, sustainability, peace and equality. These values seep into my poetry because they're such a deep part of me.

6. **What is your work ethic?**
There's a discipline to writing, like everything else. I find editing much easier to control, because it uses a different side of my brain. The creative part can be frustrating. I think, like everyone, I sometimes suffer times when I feel like I can't write anything at all. I do a lot of writing exercises, like haikus or creating 'found poems' out of newspaper cuttings, and I read a lot. It's like anything – the more you practice, the better you'll get at it.

7. **How do the writers you read when you were young influence you today?**

   Certain writers go with you all the way through your life, almost like personal friends. Herman Hesse is one. I fell in love with his short stories as a student. I live in Swansea, just around the corner from where Dylan Thomas grew up and I'd be lying if I said he wasn't a big influence. I love the way he plays with words and imagery, and his anarchic sense of humour. Angela Carter is another. I think fairytales was where it all started for me, and fiction-wise, that hasn't changed. I'm fascinated by folklore, particularly Celtic. Since living in Wales I've become aware of the Bardic tradition of interweaving music with poetry. As a writer and musician, this is something I'm keen to explore.

8. **Who of today's writers do you admire the most and why?**

   Oh gosh, there are so many, it's hard to know where to start! I read every poetry book I can get my hands on, from the well-known to emerging new writers. I've a shelf of books written by my writer friends and I read as many books by new writers as I can. Some of my favourite poets currently are Craig Raine, Carol Ann Duffy, Elizabeth Jennings. I've recently discovered Fran Lock's work and she's phenomenal – everyone should read her!

9. Why do you write, as opposed to doing anything else?

I love it! Simple as that. I sing as well, and sometimes paint, but writing has always been my overriding passion. I can't imagine not doing it. I think I'd go mad!

10. What would you say to someone who asked you "How do you become a writer?"

Don't assume that you will earn a lot of money (you probably won't). Don't try to please everybody (you can't). Don't compare yourself to others but be the best version of yourself. Try not to take rejections personally and don't be disheartened. Be kind to other writers and build one another up – it's not a competition! If you can, join an open mic or a writing group, as having a community really helps keep you inspired. Take a notebook and pen everywhere. Most of all, write, write, write.

ABOUT THE AUTHOR

Rebecca Lowe is a freelance writer, a Pushcart prize nominated poet, and a Bread and Roses Spoken Word 2020 Award winner. She is based in Swansea, Wales. Her first poetry collection, Blood and Water, was published by The Seventh Quarry Press in 2020. Her latest collection, Our Father Eclipse was published by Culture Matters in 2021. She has been published in numerous anthologies internationally and received an award of excellence at the Chinese Poetry Spring Festival. Her poetry has been translated into Welsh, Romanian, Greek, Chinese and Hindi.

NOTES:

[i] 'Deliberate Practice' – K. Anders Ericsson and Kyle W. Hartwell, (1993) www.frontiersin.org
[ii] 'We receive on average the equivalent of 100,000 new words of information every day'. 'How Much Information?' University of California and San Diego, Bohn and Short, 2009.
[iii] 'The Harmony of the Spheres: What modern physics can tell us', Professor Tamara Davis, August 2018, www.abc.net.au
[iv] 'Is Noise Always Bad? Exploring the Effects of Ambient Noise on Creative Cognition', Journal of Consumer Research Inc, Ravi Mehta, Rui Juliet Zhu, Amar Cheema, December 2012. www.researchgate.nettio
[v] 'Creativity in The Wild: Improving creativity through immersion in natural settings', Ruth Ann Atchley, David L Strayer, Paul Atchley, University of Kansas, David Strayer, University of Kansas, Dec 2012, Public Library of Science, www.journals.plos.org
[vi] Kathleen Vohs PHD University of Minnesota Carlson School of Management, September 2013, www.psychologicalscience.org
[vii] 'Fertile Green: Green Facilitates Creative Performance. Lichtenfeld S, Elliot AJ Maier MA, Pekrun R. Pers Soc Psychol. Bulletin, 2012 June. www.pubmed.ncbi.nlm.nih.gov
[viii] 'Effect of Colors: Blue Boosts Creativity, While Red Enhances Attention to Detail, Juliet Zhu, University of British Colombia's Saunder School of Business, 5 Feb 2009, Science, www.sciencedaily.com
[ix] 'The impact of physical exercise on convergent and divergent thinking', Lorenzo S Calzato, Ayca Szapora, Justine N. Pannekoek, Bernhard Hommel, Front. Hum. Neurosci. 2 December 2013, www.frontiers.org
[x] 'Specific Mindfulness Skills Differentially Predict Creative Performance', Matthijs Baas, Barbora Nevicka, Femke S Ten Velden, May 2014, Personality and Social Psychology Bulletin. www.researchgate.net

[xi] 'Handwriting but not typewriting leads to widespread brain connectivity: a high-density ECG study with imoplications for the

classroom'. Audrey van der Meer, Ruud van der Weel, Norwegian University of Science and Technology, Front. Psychol. 26 January 2024. www.frontiers.org

[xii] Based on a study by Gloria Mark, UC Irvine's Chancellor's Professor of Informatics. See www.gloriamark.com

[xiii] Pennebaker JW, 1997, 'Writing about emotional experiences as a therapeutic process', Psychological Science, 8, 162-166. www.journals.sagepub.com

[xiv] William Carlos Williams said that 'utter originality is, of course, out of the question.' This is taken from Page: The Letters of Ezra Pound: 1907-1941. Ed DD Paige, New York, Harcourt, Brace and Co, 1950; page 6. Most of my information on Imagist Poetry was learned from the 'Imagist Poetry', edited by Peter Jones, publ. Penguin Books 1972. This is an excellent introduction to imagist poetry with work from most of the major early contributors to the genre, as well as examples of poems 'before' and 'after' they were edited.

[xv] Pearl S Buck, Novelist and Nobel Laureate (1892-1973).

[xvi] 'The Shower Effect: Mind-wandering facilitates creative incubation during moderately engaging activities' Psychology of Aesthetics, Creativity an the Arts', Experimental Philosophy and Cognitive Science, Zachary C Irving, C McGrath, L Flynn, A Glasser, C Mills (2023), www.zacharycirving.com

[xvii] 'Creativity as a Neuroscientific Mystery', M. Boden, publ, MIT Press, 20 September 2013, www.semanticscholar.org

[xviii] 'Portrait of a Friend' is written by Gwen Watkins, wife of Vernon Watkins who was one of Dylan Thomas's longest-standing friends, and a fellow poet. It is published by Gomer Press, 1 July 1983. ISBN-10: 0850888476.

[xix] 'The Daily Routine of 20 Famous Writers (and How You Can Use Them to Succeed) by Mayo Oshin at www.mayooshin.com; 'How Artists Work: Daily Rituals' by Mason Currey. Publ. Knopf, 23 April 2013. ISBN-10: 0307273601. The quote by Barack Obama is from 'A Promised Land' by Barack Obama, Publ. Viking 17 Nov 2020. ISBN-10: 0241491517.

[xx] From 'Caitlin: Life With Dylan Thomas 'by Caitlin Thomas with George Tremlett, publ. Henry Holt and Co, 1 March 1987. ISBN-10: 080500369X.

[xxi] A copy of Charles Olson's essay 'Projective Verse', first published in Black Mountain Review, can be found online via www.researchgate.net (DOI:10:3390/h7040108). There is also a version on YouTube read by David Fuller.

[xxii] Mihal Csikszentmihalyi, 'Flow: The Psychology of Optimal Experience (1990), publ . Harper Perennial Modern Classics, ISBN 10-006133390202.

[xxiii] Magic Happens (inside of you) – Little Books with Big Ideas, Laurie Fisher Huck, publ. Thorsons, 1 Oct 1998. (ISBN: 9781901881097).

[xxiv] This was originally written by Neil Gaiman on Tumblr and is reposted in full on his page for Wednesday May 17 2017 at www.journal.neilgaiman.com

[xxv] The Mindful Pause comes from Dialectical Behavioural Therapy, a therapeutic technique that incorporates mindfulness into Cognitive Behavioural Therapy. The STOP technique was developed by John Kabat-Zinn, a prominent mindfulness researcher (see.www.cogbtherapy.com).

[xxvi] 'Surely You're Joking, Mr Feynman?', by Richard Feynman, publ. Vintage, 7 Jun2 1992, ASIN 009917331X.

[xxvii] The Emerald is a Podcast by Joshua Shrei. It 'explores the human experience through a vibrant lens of myth, story and imagination.' I'd thoroughly recommend it.

[xxviii] This story is recounted in www.tolkeingateway.net

[xxix] A good, simple explanation of Taoism, its history and Taoist beliefs can be found at www.sciencedirect.com 'Taoism: HG Moeller, in Encylopaedia of Applied Ethics (second Edition), 2012.'

[xxx] 'Modern Fiction' by Virginia Woolf, appears in The Broadview Anthology of British Literature: The Twentieth Century and Beyond, ed. Joseph Black, 2006. The essay is also available online at www.edisciplinas.usp.br

Printed in Great Britain
by Amazon